FEB 0 1 2

W9-CSV-093

MAKE A LIST

MAKE A LIST

How a Simple Practice Can
Change Our Lives and Open Our Hearts

MARILYN MCENTYRE

WILLIAM B. EERDMANS PUBLISHING COMPANY
Grand Rapids, Michigan

Wм. B. Eerdmans Publishing Co.
2140 Oak Industrial Drive N.E., Grand Rapids, Michigan 49505
www.eerdmans.com

27 26 25 24 23 22 21 20 19 18   1 2 3 4 5 6 7 8 9 10

ISBN 978-0-8028-7574-7

Library of Congress Cataloging-in-Publication Data

Names: McEntyre, Marilyn Chandler, 1949- author.
Title: Make a list : how a simple practice can change our lives and
    open our hearts / Marilyn McEntyre.
Description: Grand Rapids : Eerdmans Publishing Co., 2018.
Identifiers: LCCN 2017039681 | ISBN 9780802875747
    (hardcover : alk. paper)
Subjects: LCSH: Spiritual life. | Self-actualization (Psychology)—
    Religious aspects. | Lists. | Success. | Change (Psychology)
Classification: LCC BL624 .M39655 2018 | DDC 204/.4—dc23
    LC record available at https://lccn.loc.gov/2017039681

For the people who keep me on their prayer list
and their contact list.
For the people who distract me from the to-do list
and the people who help me get through it.
And for all the people on my A-list,
whose names are inscribed in my heart—
the whole long list of you.
You know who you are.

CONTENTS

Part I: Why Make a List?

Lists serve a surprising variety of purposes. Here are a few reasons to make them.

CONTENTS

Contents

Part II: The Way of the List-Maker

There aren't many "rules" in list-making, but there are reliable ways to make lists useful, beautiful, and fun. Here are a few to try out.

Contents

Part III: Play Lists

Lists are a way of opening up "play space." This section is an invitation to play—to tinker with each other's lists, to use the ones provided here as templates for your own, to move lines around and change the mood and marvel at your own ingenuity. Consider, as you read these lists and the short reflections that follow each of them, where whimsy, need, poetic inclinations, and playful imagination might take you.

Appendix: A Few Final Lists
for Your General Enjoyment

INTRODUCTION: LIVING BY LISTS

I list a lot. And I'm not alone. In the course of many kitchen-table conversations, I've discovered that we keep lists for a variety of reasons. People make lists to get organized, to plan the day, to set priorities, to clarify "pros" and "cons" as they make decisions, to explore their feelings, to dispel mental fog, to articulate goals, to identify their deepest hopes and purposes.

What I've also discovered about lists is that every time I make one, I learn something. Things come up. Sometimes it seems that the less I plan or try to foresee what might belong on a list, the more I find out. So I just start in: "Things to do before the weekend"; "Possible blog topics"; "People to get back to"; "Nagging anxieties"; "Things I'm grateful for." Even if the heading seems rather ho-hum ("Things to do") or borders on cliché ("Things to be grateful for"), the process brings surprises.

If I stay with it long enough to get beyond the obvious (buy the groceries, return the phone call, check e-mail, get the oil changed . . .), something not so obvious occurs, and the list shifts from "list" to something more: take a walk

1

by the river with no phone; pick up protein bars to keep in the car for homeless people; write to a grandchild about his science project. And I discover not only what I think I need to do, but what I want to do, what I've avoided doing, and what I don't do because I don't really want to.

This is important information. In the process of making a list, I generally find that I can, as a therapist used to advise, "go to the place in me that knows." Line by line, I can take myself there. It's a place of deep, lively, sometimes amusing, sometimes daunting encounter with the self and, often, encounter with the indwelling Spirit who is more present, available, reliable, and forgiving than we may think.

When you make a list, if you stay with it and take it slowly, take it seriously but playfully, give yourself plenty of permission to put down whatever comes up, you begin to clarify your values, your concerns, the direction your life is taking, your relationship to your inner voice, your humor, your secrets. You discover the larger things that lists can reveal.

Lists are mirrors. When you look at what you've written down, no matter what the content, a list shows you something about what has come to matter to you. Even if a phrase or a line occurs to you because you like the way it sounds, because it's funny, or because of what seems a random, interruptive thought, it's worth paying attention to. Listing, because it takes away a certain pressure to make sense, allows space for all associations. And whatever shows up, as in dreams, probably matters.

Lists are a way of learning. E. M. Forster's famous question "How can I know what I think until I see what I say?" remains an encouragement for writers to write and provides a lively incentive to undertake even the humble task of making a list. List-making almost always leads to surprises. We "find ourselves" remembering a scene or recognizing a problem or identifying a hope that hadn't occurred to us until that moment. Writing down one sentence or phrase or sometimes even a single word opens a door and invites what's been held just below the boundaries of consciousness to come forward. Those surprises are key learning moments. We learn a little more about ourselves, our values, the changes that are occurring in this season of life. We also recognize fluctuations of feeling as we add things to the list that make us aware of desires, inhibitions, anxieties, currents of restlessness, and curiosities we hadn't noticed before.

Lists are a way of listening. As we add lines to a list, we become aware of the voice in us that speaks when we listen. This is an experience I often have in prayer or meditation: a sentence or a phrase "comes" from somewhere other than my busy ego-mind. I experience it as a gift received. Poets and people who work in other creative arts often speak of how a line or an image or an idea "just came to me" in the course of painting or writing or sculpting.

In order for that to happen, a person has to remain open to the new and the unplanned even in the midst of a project—something that can be difficult for very goal-oriented people. But even for the more driven, a list can be a simple way of pausing and allowing, making space for more when the mind might begin to close or clutch at a single plan too soon. It's a reminder that there's always more to see or to listen for. It slows the scampering mind and tempers argument with imagination. Inevitably, a line or two on a lengthening list will resonate with possibility. Those lines may surprise and summon us to approaches we hadn't imagined before. Something in the momentum of list-making opens corners of the mind that can be hard to reach and gives the inner voice a say.

Lists are a way of loving. Paying attention is the first step toward love. We can love only what we notice, name, return to, and reflect on. Listing is a way of calling to our own attention those things that might have lingered at the margins of our awareness, giving them a place as we re-order our priorities. As I made the list "When to call home" (Part III), I added, as they occurred to me, lines like "When it's too early to call anyone else" and "When you wish to be celebrated" and "When you need a reality check"—and realized with renewed gratitude and a rush of affection how much I loved the people at home who would answer that call. If I list what I love about my daughter, dimensions of her life I rarely pause to consider become more apparent, and the mystery of her own otherness renews my awareness that even those we think we know best are complex, mysterious beings, put into our lives for purposes we can't fully fathom, and finally known only to God. Many of the poems I've written for my husband began as lists. What occurred to me this Valentine's Day was to thank him for the way he brings color into my life through his paintings, in the flowers he chooses for the garden, in his bright shirts and the wild dragons he draws with our grandson. Considering all that color gave me one more way to appreciate the gift that he is.

Lists are a way of letting go. When oppressive memories and nagging fears or anxieties keep our throats tight, our stomachs aching, or our muscles clenched, a list can be a helpful instrument of release. As we put down and look at what we've held on to a little too tightly for a little too long, whether it's inscribed on paper or glowing on a screen where the "delete" button lies ready at hand, we may find that we've already allowed ourselves to let go a little. We may find that what looms and threatens may not be quite so unmanageable as we thought. To identify what we feel, as specifically as possible, when someone we find difficult or threatening enters the room can help us prepare and protect ourselves as we strive to keep and make peace. That's what a list can do.

It can also name what we miss in a season of loss. It can become a ritual of release as we pause over each cherished aspect of a beloved person who is gone, or over each familiar place in a home that we've left. We allow ourselves to feel the ache but also put to rest what needs to be given back to time and memory and God so that we can continue our journeys a little freer of the undertow that impedes our ability to dwell fully in the present.

Lists may become a prayer practice. I didn't grow up praying the rosary or the long litanies that some churches still recite on solemn or festive occasions. Indeed, my father was of the generation of Christians who held hard to biblical warnings against "vain repetition." It wasn't until I reached early adulthood and sat among people who patiently spoke a repeated refrain—"Have mercy on us" or "Pray for us" or "Graciously hear us"—that I experienced the way a litany, which balances changing focus with grounding repetition, can gentle the mind into a deep place of meditation and soften the heart into receptivity. To write out our specific petitions followed by a refrain or to write down the names of those we invoke to help us can add a valuable dimension to our practice of the presence of God. To list our longings or the causes of our anguish or reasons to rejoice can clarify and enhance the conversations we have with the Spirit and the self and shine new light on paths that sometimes take us through the shadows.

These are just a few of the many purposes that list-making can serve. The following pages are an invitation to explore these purposes further. Each section offers prompts for those who want to play with the many possibilities open to the interested list-maker. As you move from one section to the next, I hope that you'll be induced to take the invitation personally and that, now and then, you'll be led to put this book down long enough to add lines to your own lengthening lists.

In Part I, I provide a series of reflections on the purposes and pleasures of list-making. Here we'll consider how list-making can become not only a useful habit, but a means of growth—even a kind of spiritual discipline. Once you give a list some space in a notebook and some time in your day, new shoots of awareness and buds of ideas begin to appear. And your purposes may change over time. What began as a simple enumeration of tasks may lead to an inventory of distractions from which you'd like to free yourself. What began as a list of annoyances may become an agenda for a much-needed and long-postponed conversation. What began as an exercise in gratitude may grow into a prayer.

In Part II, I offer more specific reflections on particular life situations in which lists may become instruments of illumination or direction or discernment. While list-making requires no particular occasion, certain occasions lend themselves to the practice: celebrations, losses, new loves, campaigns, relocations, beginnings, and farewells—all these deserve the long pause that allows for articulation.

Holiday rituals and life transitions can easily fall into cliché, but can be revived and renewed by the simple practice of speaking the small truths that animate the abstractions. It's sweet to hear "I love you" on Valentine's Day, but the message can become even more meaningful when it's accompanied by a list of "Things I love about you" or "Moments that have made me fall in love with you again." At Thanksgiving, it's good to go around the table and let each person in turn offer one thing he or she is thankful for. But one year it might be refreshing—and revealing—to vary the ritual by having everyone put together a list of "Ways I like to be thanked."

In Part III, I offer a number of my lists, written on a variety of occasions, along with stories about how they grew. My hope is that in reading through my lists you'll feel encouraged to make your own, to tinker with them, to let them grow up to be poems or essays or love letters or blog posts. I have found, over time, that lines from my lists remain in my memory as reminders or benchmarks or signposts. Some have ended up on my wall. Some have become birthday cards. Some have remained on scraps of paper I come across now and then, tucked into books or the backs of drawers, and rediscovering them, like finding money in a pocket, has provided moments of unexpected satisfaction.

Wherever your lists turn up, I hope they will offer occasional epiphanies, foster conversations worth having, and become gifts for you and others.

Part I

WHY MAKE A LIST?

Since the purposes that lists serve are so various, this section offers some reflections on particular kinds of lists and the insights and satisfactions they can provide. Naming what we want, what we feel, what we're afraid of, naming the uncertainties or delights or questions that come to mind in the moment can help us take stock of our own shifting priorities, our progress or growth in certain areas, and where we may need to re-awaken and pay closer attention to what we've sidelined. Lists beget other lists, as do questions. There are scores of answers to "Why Make a List?" Here are a few.

To discover subtle layers of feeling

List-making slows you down. You may find your pen hovering in the air above the page or your fingers resting before returning to the keyboard as you ponder what you just put down. You hadn't realized you felt that way. You hadn't known what rush of memory a particular word would trigger—perhaps a well-concealed wistfulness about a road not taken, or an edgy uncertainty about something you haven't fully faced, or an unexpected delight that motivates you to explore further something you may have been postponing for a more opportune time. This may be that time.

When I wrote a list entitled "What love looks like," for instance, I began to realize and appreciate in new ways the kinds of attention I'd received from people over the years who I wouldn't have said loved me, but who enhanced my life and learning in ways I now indeed would call love. "A babysitter building a block tower," "A white-haired woman in the picket line," "A seventh-grade soccer coach on Saturday morning"—all embody a kind of generosity and care for others' welfare that links love to kindness, justice, and patience.

The great definition of love in 1 Corinthians 13, recited at many weddings but meant as a general guide for loving life and each other all the time, includes these lines: "Love is patient and kind; love does not envy or boast; it is not arrogant or rude. It does not insist on its own way; it is not irritable or resentful; it does not rejoice at wrongdoing, but rejoices in the truth." As I made my list, those lines came to mind, and along with them, recollections of occasions when someone showed me what patience, kindness, humility, and good-humored grace look like in the flesh. That list led me down pathways of gratitude I had never fully explored.

As I wrote a line about a grandpa reading, I found myself smiling over the image, since so much of the love I experienced as a child happened as I snuggled onto someone's lap or leaned into a shoulder and listened to a story. And as it occurred to me to include "a monk at prayer" in the list of those who embody love, I thought of all the quiet, unobtrusive, faithful people I have known who have lit my path with love in ways I barely recognized until later.

The act of making this list makes me newly aware of dimensions of love I rarely recognize—quiet sacrifice, willingness to correct, exuberance, attention to details, laughter. The feelings that arose in the process were the reward for this little exercise. As with many of the lists I look back on, this one seems to offer a kind of archaeological record of emotions felt and refined over the years into more nuanced, rich, colorful experiences.

What love looks like

A seventh-grade soccer coach on Saturday morning
A night nurse changing bandages
A teacher tutoring at lunchtime
A worried parent at three a.m.
A white-haired woman in a picket line
A grandpa reading a storybook instead of the
     evening paper
A vet who talks to the kitty
A monk at prayer
A babysitter building a block tower
A donor at the blood bank
A husband brewing coffee at six a.m.
A volunteer cutting carrots in the soup kitchen
A sister listening to late-night laments
A mom who says no and finds a yes to go with it
A policy-maker who remembers the poor

SOME LISTS TO TRY:

Seven kinds of satisfaction
What's underneath the anger
What happens in the aftermath
Feelings I tend to suppress
When I am most content

TO NAME WHAT YOU WANT

Knowing what you want isn't as simple or obvious a matter as it might seem. You might fall into a restless, itchy state of discontent or a vague, unspecified wanting during which you find yourself musing in front of an open refrigerator or closet or door, wondering what satisfaction would look like. That kind of unfocused wanting is a very common problem—particularly among those of us who live in conditions of chronic choice overload.

One solution to that problem may be a list. Pen in hand, line by line, you can get from "I don't know what I want" to "I know I want these things." It's like moving out of a confusing fog into a clear landscape of possibility. Once you know what you want (even if you think you shouldn't want it, and have therefore been repressing the wanting), the next steps become clearer. If it's a vacation, you can check the calendar, review your cash flow, and begin to plan. If it's learning to swing dance, you can look for local classes online and consider how to make room for lessons in your life. If it's a closer relationship with your spouse, you can make an occasion for the conversation you've been postponing, or a special dinner just for the two of you. If it's a deeper spiritual life, you can make a list (!) of

13

the books others have recommended, or take a day at a retreat center or an hour at a lakeside for quiet prayer or meditation. Whatever your wants, listing them can not only give direction but also unleash the energy you need to move in that direction.

Of course, wants change over time, sometimes without our fully realizing it. It may dawn upon us gradually that the car we thought we were "saving up for" or the trip we hoped to take before older age is no longer appealing. Now we find ourselves with other wants. They may be focused less on things and more on making time and space for friendship, developing dormant talents, learning new skills, finding companionship in conversation, nurturing our spiritual growth. Or it may be that persistent desires we have dismissed as trivial deserve some attention: a new hairstyle, a different color on the walls, raised beds in the garden, the one piece of jewelry it's always felt excessive to ask for, conversation with a growing child about something we rarely broach.

I recognize that my wants have changed over the past decade; they're simpler in some ways, more focused on less—fewer commitments, fewer things to take care of—and clearer about desires I would call "inner" or "spiritual"—time, space, silence, reflection, time with friends. Here's a recent list:

What I want now

Quiet companionship
Good walking shoes
Candlelight every evening
Good coffee every morning
Time to read
And reread
Energy to care for those who need my care
Podcasts worth pondering
Suppers and song with people I love

This list included lines that, as they occurred to me, helped me recognize that shift. And I realized that I already had some of these things, which made me aware again of a simple, lovely, useful definition of contentment: wanting what you have.

The "Now" is an important part of this list's title. Noticing how wants change is important information for us and for those who know us best. It's so easy to think we have ourselves or our loved ones "pegged." But they can surprise us, and we can surprise ourselves. That's why naming wants can be revelatory. We discover that we want something we hadn't quite bothered—or been brave enough—to identify. We find ourselves wanting with more wistfulness or urgency or eagerness than we had realized.

These wants inspire other variants of the "What I want"

list: "What I want right now"; "What I want but hesitate to ask for"; "What I want but am embarrassed to ask for"; "What I want to want"; "What I wish I didn't want"; "What I want for the people I love." It's important to consider these and other explorations of wanting as a dimension of inner life. The more we list various kinds of wants, the more we discover that desire itself is a life force. The blissful state of wanting nothing may be a valuable ideal and a mark of spiritual advancement, but it's unlikely that we'll be able even to approximate that kind of holy contentment without first and fully acknowledging the desires that drive us, sometimes getting us into trouble, sometimes teaching us. Knowing the good we *do* want can temper and direct these desires, and is a helpful step in learning what we *should* want. It's part of the process of learning to want the best things, of educating our desires.

Of course, even when we bring all this awareness to our wanting, we may not get everything we want. But knowing what we want helps us consider what's possible and also recognize what we may simply need to let go of. I may want to learn to make and glaze a pot, but given all the other things I want, that may just not happen. So I'll admire other people's pots and go on with my limited life. Lists help me do that. They also help fuel hopes, showing us that there are any number of things we can learn and try and enjoy more fully. To look them in the face is to greet them, in a way, and to honor them, and to move in their direction.

SOME LISTS TO TRY:

Things I've begun wanting recently
Things I've wanted for the last five minutes
Things I've wanted for more than five years
Things I want for the next generation
Things I'd like to stop wanting

TO CLARIFY YOUR CONCERNS

Whether or not you set out to make a list of current concerns, as soon as you set out to make a list at all, they're likely to come up. When you make a list, you open a space in which things can bubble up from where they've lain trapped in pockets under the surface of consciousness. Fears, especially, often go unnamed because they're hard to face and easy to hide behind the false comfort of denial. Guilt and regret also get pushed underground, and anxieties about others' lives that we can't do much about, and discontents that seem a little dangerous to explore. So, for example, my current list of concerns might look something like this:

This season's concerns

The dying of a dear one
Information overload
Climate change and carbon footprints
A friend's divorce
My spouse's discouragements
And my own
How to find time for what I treasure
And silence enough to renew my spirit

When I look at my own list of concerns, I see more clearly how the tectonic shifts in American public life affect my personal life, directly and daily, as I decide how much of the *Times* to read, whether I have a whole hour for *Democracy Now!,* how many petitions to sign or phone calls to make to my senators, when to write an op-ed piece, and when to let it all go, look around, be local, be humbly, simply present, and lean into the sun so I can bloom where I'm planted.

Making a list of current concerns can also help us notice where our energies tend to flow as we live and move among people we love—how others' losses, illnesses, and fluctuations of fortune affect us. We may be led once again to reflect on the importance of strengthening personal boundaries, for instance, or on the difference between generous sympathy and anxious hovering.

In the list above, for example, I included "a friend's divorce," recognizing how deeply her pain and her husband's tugged at my heart, and at the same time how important it was that I confine my concerns for the most part to prayer and availability. They needed space and time to work out their differences—not the "help" I might too readily be inclined to offer. So I refrained from calling to ask how it was going, which was a challenge for me. But naming it on my list of concerns gave it a place on my "mattering map" and reminded me I could own the concern without having to quell it by acting in ways that suited my needs rather than theirs. Even "my spouse's discouragements," which I witness at much closer range than those of my friends, are not, finally, my own. As I include them on my list of concerns, I am again aware of my own need for ongoing discernment about when to "help" and when to let him walk, pray, wrestle, and reflect until he's ready to talk.

These lists are where we get explicit with ourselves: each item nudges us toward candor and clarity. They put our concerns in sharper focus and motivate us to address them in healthy and thoughtful ways, helping us find and hold appropriate distances. And naming our concerns allows us not only to revisit them but to revise them in in ways that funnel them into prayer or action, or simply allows us to lay them down gently and, as my mother often put it, "Give them to God."

Some of our concerns we can address on our own; some we need others' help with; some only God can manage. Naming them, specifying them, seeing them before us on the page, can help us distinguish which is which.

SOME LISTS TO TRY:

Concerns about [a particular loved one]
Who is attending to public concerns I care about
Undue pressures on young people I love
When to speak out
How to sustain my own mental/emotional health

To decide what to let go of

The matter of what to let go of can be an offshoot of naming what you want, but it also merits its own discussion because it's a list that may need rewriting with surprising frequency. No doubt all of us are intimately familiar with our own specific tendencies to "clutch and cling." So tackling this particular list can help us open our hands and hearts and the corners of the mind that fold down over whatever is difficult to release. It can be a hard list to make, but the result can be very freeing.

At a women's retreat I led a while back, I suggested that the participants try making a list of "Things to Let Go Of." One woman responded immediately, with a note of alarm in her voice, "I don't think I want to do that!" Everyone else laughed because her hesitation struck a familiar note. Part of the reason letting go is so difficult is that it's a lesson we keep getting, and learning, over and over as we let go of homes, children, jobs, social commitments we no longer have time for, possessions we have no room for, relationships that have ceased to be life-giving. At every season of life—and often more frequently—we have to shed some things. That becomes increasingly apparent as we live longer and realize that living is a long process of receiving and letting go, one gift relinquished to make room for the next. In-breath and out-breath.

But though we may recognize the frequency and necessity of it, the letting-go part remains difficult, especially in this culture where we continue, to our collective detriment, to measure success and comfort by accumulation (not only of stuff, but of titles, memberships, degrees, social contacts, and Facebook "friends"). Even letting go of things or habits that we know to be distractions, that our wiser self recognizes we'd be better off without, can feel hard or threatening. "What am I clinging to?" is a useful question to ask ourselves from time to time. Or "What's cluttering my days or sapping my energies, and how might it feel to be free of it?" This kind of liberation takes both clarity and courage.

My first serious engagement with the question of what to let go of came in high school when I read Thoreau's *Walden*. "Simplicity, simplicity, simplicity," he urges, and in his clever, curmudgeonly way goes on for some two hundred pages advocating a life that is closer to nature, more attuned to the seasons, and free of the possessions that "possess us." Among his many oft-quoted lines about the dangers of acquisition and accumulation is one that still makes me smile when I occasionally see it inscribed on a student's T-shirt: "Beware of all enterprises that require new clothes." I don't live alone in a one-room cabin, and unlike Jesus, I have a rather comfortable place to lay my head every night. But the challenging call to consider the lilies and clean out the garage remains an essential guideline in decisions about acquisition and a valuable point of reference when I ask myself why I hold on and when to let go.

Here's my version:

Things to let go of

The flute lessons I don't have time for
Perpetual political outrage
Anxieties about adult children's adult problems

Last week's casserole
Because, really, no one is going to eat it
All hope of learning Russian
Hospice patients I've come to love
Friends whose going I can hardly bear
Yesterday's mistakes

Some of the listed items make me smile, albeit wryly: decades into adult life, I still harbor the delusion that someone will suddenly devour the leftovers I don't actually want, but hate to see "go to waste." Some of the items make me sigh. I'd still like to play the flute and read Tolstoy in his native tongue. But writing the lines above has allowed me to pause long enough to imagine that I might not have to let go altogether. Perhaps I could give up the hope of flute mastery and enjoy playing some very simple tunes, or learn a Russian song from a child I know who sings them. And some of the items on my let-go list open deep veins of sorrow and serious reflection. Deaths come, and every ultimate letting go is its own reminder of mortality and mystery. We let go because we must. We also learn, with God's help, and the help of the wisest among us, to do it with grace and hope.

SOME LISTS TO TRY:

What needs reclassification as clutter
What to give away to whom
What is no longer useful to me
What old resentments I can relinquish
Where I still need to accept forgiveness

TO HELP DISPEL A FEW FEARS

Denial of fear runs deep. It's not uncommon these days to run into people who have reached their limit in conversations about climate change or threats to family life or contaminated food or gun violence. Simply identifying fears can be scary: the more specific we get about what we're afraid of, the more threatening it may seem. Or the more powerless we may feel.

But the value of naming fears is that some may be dispelled with a little more information, and that even the big ones that don't go away may be shared or addressed more meaningfully. We may not be able to do much about the threats posed by extremist groups or about the reckless drivers on the freeways our favorite teens are learning to navigate, but if we name those fears, we're more likely to look up groups who are addressing them on the level of policy, legislation, and public education. And making a list of fears can be a way of affirming the truth that facing fear is a way of choosing life—choosing to trust in the Power that protects us, in the power of communal action, and the power of awareness.

I turn and face, for instance, these fears:

What I'm afraid of

Local and international violence
Drought and other devastations of climate change
A food system that puts public health at risk
Routine risks that children and grandchildren take
Surveillance
Power-mongering leaders
And timid ones
Mental decline that comes with age
Being misunderstood
Being misrepresented
Losing the ones I love

As I look at my own list, I see how many of my fears are large-scale these days—unsurprising, I suppose, as global tensions persist and become more complicated and change accelerates. In this season of my life, I'm very much aware that I'm no longer as deeply imbedded in family or institutional responsibilities as I used to be, and so I have the freedom to take a good look at the bigger picture, read the *New York Times*, sign petitions, talk with friends about matters of public concern, and attend book groups. So the focus of my fears has become wider. Some of them even seem apocalyptic.

But such fears are nothing new. I remember trying to go to sleep as a child in a room next to the one where my parents watched the ten o'clock news. I remember Walter Cronkite's voice, and a crackly version of Krushchev's as he banged his shoe on the U.N. desk and threatened, "We will bury you!" I remember bomb drills and revelations about DDT and the first time I read an article predicting global warming. I don't remember my fears ever being confined to personal dangers, though I was a little afraid of barking dogs and car accidents on the L.A. freeways.

When I look at my list, I also see that my own death isn't there. That omission I attribute to my mother. She saw many people die in her work with a medical team in Indian villages and again later when she served various church communities as a deacon and a sort of one-woman hospice volunteer. Though she could enter with empathy into others' sadness, she accepted death. To her, it meant going home to God. The hope she invested in that prospect was so real and so grounded that I received and internalized it as part of her legacy. There were things to be afraid of, but death, at least my death, was not one of them.

But that clarity and confidence about death didn't do away with other ordinary human fears. I am afraid of pain. And loss. And accidents and natural disasters and personal conflict. In our family's culture, I sometimes felt hesitant as a child to say I was afraid. So it's been good for me to explore those very real fears. Claiming permission to be afraid rather than simply berating myself for lacking faith, not praying or trusting enough, took some time. The many moments in Bible stories when an angel or Jesus begins an encounter with "Be not afraid" can seem like prohibition. But those greetings are also, and perhaps more importantly, compassionate acknowledgments of very human fears, and gentle offers to dispel those fears.

Still, they can't be dispelled until they're named. Slow, vivid, specific, sometimes painful naming of fears is the beginning of letting them go. Letting the list grow, giving it all the space it needs, can be an effective strategy of self-healing that sometimes allows us, as Wendell Berry puts it, to "be joyful though you have considered all the facts." The facts generally include some good news: competent people are working on solutions; faith communities and families are reaching out with grace and imagination to help those in particular need; what seem to be failing systems sometimes prove surprisingly resilient. And where good news seems scarce, listing the fears can sometimes drive us deeper into prayers that pave a pathway to trust.

SOME LISTS TO TRY:

Fears for the children I care about
Ways of addressing my favorite fears
Changes I find threatening
"Irrational" fears
Texts that help me with my fears

TO CLAIM WHAT GIVES YOU JOY

I recently read the surprisingly popular, slightly odd book called *The Life-Changing Magic of Tidying Up* by Marie Kondo. Among other enthusiastic suggestions for decluttering domestic space, she advises her readers to pick up each thing they own, hold it, and consider whether it gives them joy. If it doesn't give you joy, she insists, let it go. Even if you paid a lot for it. Even if someone you don't want to offend gave it to you. Keep only those things that give you joy.

It seems hard to apply this bit of wisdom to food storage containers or the office supplies in the bottom desk drawer. My extra potato peelers don't give me joy. Holiday ads notwithstanding, more merchandise doesn't make me more joyful, and even my favorite possessions, though they give me satisfaction and pleasure, are rarely responsible for my experiences of real joy. But Kondo's general idea is a good one: pay attention to what helps you choose life and live it joyfully, and let go of whatever inhibits that freedom of spirit.

Joy is a big three-letter word. Although it often seems overused and sometimes trivialized in certain kinds of churchy conversation, it retains a biblical lineage that reminds us to imagine something bigger than ordinary pleasure or happiness—heart-opening delight in the good gifts that surprise us beyond our too-limited expectations. Or the deep well-being that comes from dwelling secure in the presence of the Beloved—the kind the Psalmist refers to when he writes, "In your presence is the fullness of joy." In fact, such biblical references abound: one is "clothed" with joy, "filled" with it, "satisfied" with it "as with a rich feast." It is often coupled with a word I like even better: *gladness.* Rejoice and be glad, the Bible tells us. Or it describes God's people as "joyful and glad of heart."

To list what makes us joyful and glad of heart—not once and for all, but at frequent intervals, reflecting on what endures and what changes in the current of our lives—is a way of stoking the fire within us and help-ing it to burn more brightly. Here's my list—for the moment:

What gives me joy

Conversation with those I love
Early morning light
Walks by water—river, lake, or ocean
Flute, fiddle, and drums
Deep quiet
The teaching that comes in dreams
Writing time
Grace, intelligence, and good humor
Stories, popcorn, and candlelight

I notice that in writing down what gives me joy, I become aware of how many things actually do.

If we think about it, we realize we could make many lists about joy. We could name each person we cherish, each author who has awakened our imagination, each ac-tivity that stirs the senses or stretches the mind or gives us practice in some life skill we're still learning. We may begin to see how joy moves among ordinary things like a breeze. We may also see how joy can be a habit of mind: the more we see how it occurs in the midst of ordinary moments on ordinary days, the more likely we are to recognize how utterly available it is—just on the other side of the veil, even in the darkest of times.

And we do live in dark times. Finding what gives us joy and naming it is a simple but significant way of keeping joy alive, and a reminder, every day, to give thanks.

SOME LISTS TO TRY:

What happens on my best days
How to enjoy what I have
Small things that make her/him glad
What I know now about happiness
How to decommercialize Christmas

TO FIND OUT WHAT YOU STILL HAVE TO LEARN

Learning, as I've discovered in my many years of trying to help others do it, can be painful as well as (see above) joyful. The painful part comes in the process of identifying uncertainties and complexities in what we thought was seamless and settled—that the dark side of American history wasn't addressed in the eighth-grade textbook, for instance. Or that translation is never exact. Or that economic "growth" means different things to different people. Or that soil is a living substance and can die.

My first days in graduate school offered me a new occasion for learning that my learning was incomplete. I'd never heard the word "intertextuality," for instance. I didn't know why the Japanese tradition of linked poetry might matter to a Western reader. And I hadn't given much thought to the political conditions under which Jane Austen wrote her novels.

But moments of discovering insufficiencies in my knowing, and in my ways of knowing, haven't been confined to classrooms. I have learned from one daughter things I never knew about proper sautéing, from another about what it takes to make sure a Cub Scout meeting isn't a waste of everyone's time, and from another a bit about the complexities of union negotiations. I've learned many things from my husband, including how to appreciate abstract expressionist art and Ella Fitzgerald. He also taught me what was lacking in the attitudes toward money I acquired growing up in a family where money was scarce.

Identifying the gaps—or oversimplifications, incompletions, ambiguities, or anomalies—in those things we think we know is certainly a good exercise in humility, but it can also be exhilarating. Every gap opens a door to new learning, and gives us a chance to practice what the Buddhists beautifully call "beginner's mind." Through those gaps, though some may open what seem to be frightening abysses of unknowing, the world can once again seem "vast and beautiful and new."

Here, as an example, is my own recent effort to identify some of the shadowy areas I haven't explored in the familiar territory of my own mind:

Where I find holes in my comfortable certainties

In moments when even those I know best mystify me
Where I see that my notion of "normal" isn't
When I experience kinds of healing that American medicine misses
When I recognize what Muslims might teach the rest of us about prayer
When I read about how gender assignment happens
When I connect dots that change the whole map

It's dangerous, I've discovered, ever to think we're done knowing—especially when we think we have someone "pegged" or when we mistake our orthodoxies for the "whole truth," since truth can only be wholly understood from God's eye-view. It's deadening not to be open to surprise precisely where we think no surprises remain.

It seems to me that a valuable part of our ongoing examinations of conscience lies in identifying what we don't know yet, but would like to, or where our notions may be oversimplified, or where we've been slothfully satisfied with sound bites. Occasionally I hear myself offer an opinion (and I have some) in a dinner-table conversation, and am startled to hear in the response an idea that actually modifies what I thought I knew. Our party loyalties need to be challenged and our certainties destabilized—even the ones we take most seriously. Because truth is like light: it casts many colors, reveals itself differently in different contexts, and is constant, subtle, mysterious, and not to be nailed down.

SOME LISTS TO TRY:

Things I'd like to know about my bioregion
Things I'd like to understand about the Bible
Things I'd like to understand about Islam
Where ignorance gets dangerous
Questions I'd like to ask [name your expert here]

TO PUT NEW WORDS TO OLD EXPERIENCES

We all develop and rely on a limited repertoire of words and phrases for most purposes. That's how we fall into language grooves and habits—and sometimes clichés. But once you begin a list, chances are you start to like the way it sounds, and you find yourself experimenting and playing with words in new ways. You might start crafting lines that are punchy or poetic, that play off each other and surprise both writer and reader with unlikely intrusions or thoughts that come in at odd angles. Now the list begins to act like a poem; the rhythm of its lines may be pleasing, and the impulse to alliterate (which I rarely resist) gathers momentum. So listing becomes, almost without effort, an exercise in word-play.

As in poetry, simple parameters shape the list. You want a single line to do its own work. One line leads to another, and you notice a certain logical progression emerging, even if the logic is oblique. As new items come to mind, the tone begins to shift, and the texture becomes more complex. Some lines will be playful, some will emerge from a place of serious concern, some will amplify the line before, some will offer an allusion that widens the frame. The words themselves become part of the fun.

And as in poetry, the shape the list begins to take and the direction it begins to go gain their own momentum. So when I set out to write a list on "The purposes of poetry," I found it beginning to act like a poem. When I added

35

stanza breaks, it acted even more like a poem. Certain lines suggested parallel and complementary lines; one allusion evoked another. The result was something very like a poem, satisfying in just the ways some poems satisfy. It gave me some new ideas to ponder about poems.

I'm accustomed to reading and talking about poetry because it's what I was trained to do. But any familiar experience bears revisiting, and, if you bring a spirit of play to it, it's likely to yield new ways of framing old stories. So, for instance, if any of us wrote a list about "The ambivalences of adolescence" or "Real truths about rude people" or "Secret pleasures," we might find, as we revisit our memories, that some of them are worth seeing in a new light.

The purposes of poetry

To find a way of putting what can't be said
To startle us into seeing
To train words to dance

To rescue worthy words from slow death
To reassert the power of whim
To combat mind erosion

To make us feel what we think
And vice versa
To resuscitate the media-impaired

Why Make a List?

To remind us that truth is round with holes and corners
To notice what will never happen just that way again
To make us consider how our light is spent

Or that the world is too much with us
Or petals on a wet black bough

SOME LISTS TO TRY:

What lay just outside the photo frame
Unhelpful euphemisms
Other answers—besides "Fine"—to "How are you?"
Phrases worth remembering
Words I've never thought to use to describe my father

TO GET AT THE QUESTIONS
BEHIND THE QUESTIONS

Somewhere I learned to begin a research project with a list of twenty-five questions about the topic. Then I would whittle down the list of questions by considering which were most inviting, intriguing, helpful—which ones gave me energy and made me want to find out more. Next I would take one of those and write five questions it raised. Say the topic is "Food in Public Schools," and one of the twenty-five questions is "What are the objections to public-school contracts with fast-food companies?" You might raise further questions like these: "Who's objecting?" "What are their alternatives?" "What leverage do those groups have?" Behind every "first question" there are always more questions. Each one is a trailhead, leading down a new path of investigation or reflection.

A good friend of mine taught me to look for the questions behind my own questions by asking me, when I mused about a matter of current concern in my life, "What's the question behind that question? What are you really asking? What is it you might really be wanting to know?" She wasn't implying that my questions were insincere or superficial, but that if I paused over them I might discover where they came from—and she was right. It's a good practice just to ask "Why might this question be coming up at this point?" or "How does my question, even unanswered, give me valuable information about what I need to be noticing: fears, hopes, turning points, what in my life is emerging, what is diminishing?"

A list that begins with a question can give birth to questions that come from a different level of awareness, "behind" or "below" the stratum of consciousness we inhabit in our waking hours. Most of us use the term "deeper" to refer to those places of mind and heart we don't usually access, and may even avoid. A simple way to go "deeper" is to ask, "What am I *really* wanting to know?" or "Why has this come to matter to me *now*?" or, alternatively, "How might this question be diverting my attention from a question I'm avoiding asking?" Getting behind our own questions in this way can lead to rich examinations of conscience and journeys of self-awareness.

Such a practice can also help us keep our faith, our intellectual growth, our relationships, and our work in the world alive and authentic. It might be a valuable exercise to write a list of questions for a personal catechism—the questions you'd write for someone just like you at your stage in life that would open doors to deeper exploration of faith. Or a list of questions that map your current curiosities—the sort of questions that might lead you to take a course in Mandarin or particle physics or wood-carving or herbal medicine.

In *Letters to a Young Poet,* Rainer Maria Rilke urges the youth to "live the questions," trusting that by doing so he might someday live out the answers. I take that mysterious advice to mean giving questions time to open up, sprout new questions, reword themselves, and direct our attention in new ways as we dwell with them and on them for a time. One common practice is to ask the same question three consecutive nights just before sleep, inviting insight to come in dreams or in the morning after the question has had a chance to sink into the unconscious or be delivered to the Spirit who guides us. If nothing else, the three days allow time for the question to "ripen." And sometimes, just by asking the question and giving it time and space, we find that we already know the answer, and that all we needed was to allow the question to take clear shape and perhaps become less scary. After that, we may be ready to go where it leads.

In *Night,* his Holocaust memoir, Elie Wiesel says of one of his mentors, "He explained to me with great insistence that every question possessed a power that did not lie in the answer." Drawing upon that teaching, he later wrote, "I pray to the God within me that he will give me the strength to ask Him the right questions." At any given moment, the "right" questions are those that direct us toward deeper awareness, livelier awakeness, keener appreciation of and empathy for others' situations, and a stronger will to see and understand.

To ask a real question, you need to be willing to hear the answer with an open heart. Listing questions is one good way to discover where the "real" questions lie. So when you consider the list below of "lists to try," imagine what one of them might open up—even if it's a can of worms—and allow each entry to lead you to a list of questions rather than answers. It might turn out that one of them is an invitation.

SOME LISTS TO TRY:

What I wonder about my work
What's been changing this year?
What's drying up or dying out and why?
Is this problem my responsibility?
What am I willing to know?

TO FIND OUT WHO'S INSIDE

One of my brightest and most memorable students was given to thinking out loud about her thoughts. She would often recount her inner dialogues with an amusing account of the conversation. "So I said to myself, 'Self, what if you looked at it this way?'" For her, thinking was clearly—even fancifully—a dialogue with the Self who lived in her and with her and vetted her ideas and questioned her motives and laughed at her pretensions and offered her a second opinion. Discovering new layers or facets of one's own psyche is a lifelong pursuit. What Jung considered the "real Self," an entity he designated with a capital S, some of us might call the soul. It is, in any case, the one within who knows the things we suppress or avoid, who has access to deep, even divine wisdom which our ego selves often miss while swimming around on the surface of consciousness, afraid to do the deep diving.

Consciousness-raising workshops and spiritual retreats and personality inventories invite us to approach and explore that deep place and meet there a Self we still know only incompletely. Discovering "who's inside" may involve us in self-examinations that aren't entirely welcome; we may have to relinquish our favorite illusions about who we are and recognize our compensations, evasions, unhealed wounds, and unresolved guilt. But for that very reason, the journey of discovery is worth making; it is hard but healing work.

The therapist I mentioned earlier—who often gently suggested, in the midst of my unsettled musings, that I go to "the place in you that knows"—simply, unquestioningly assumed that there was such a "place" in me. Soon I began to have occasional dreams (which have continued intermittently over the years) in which an older woman, or sometimes three older women, appeared, bringing some kind of guidance, direction, or encouragement. I couldn't always remember exactly what the women told me, but I generally woke up with a sense that I had within me what I needed to meet the next challenge.

Sometimes we receive such guidance in the form of a feeling: a restlessness or an impulse to act or simply a physical symptom that won't go away until we ask what it's about. Sometimes it seems to come from without—a sentence, an awareness, or a sudden noticing we didn't invent or invite. Always, if we pause over these moments, we can learn something about "who's inside."

The part of us that waits to be discovered may be drawn out by naming what lies at the outer edge of consciousness, in our peripheral vision, as it were—flickers of anxiety that keep coming up, a sense of inexplicable dissatisfaction, a recurring curiosity about something we haven't investigated, a hunger for a different kind of companionship, or little surges of pleasure in small things that might be invitations to dig a little deeper and see what vein of joy lies just beneath the surface.

The "digging" may be done one line at a time. So, for instance, if I want to understand "who's inside," I might ask myself, "Self, what have I not noticed enough?" And that Self, gratified finally to have my attention, might reply:

How your stomach hurts when you're stressed
When you need to stretch
Where you put your irritations while you're trying
    to be nice
What really gives you peace
When your heart opened a little wider

SOME LISTS TO TRY:

What choices do I make when I have a few hours alone?
Where would I go for refreshment and renewal
if I could?
What dream images stay with me?
What irritants might I need to explore?
What takes me close to tears?

TO PLAY WITH POSSIBILITIES

I've always been slightly annoyed when someone solemnly insists, in the name of broadmindedness, "There are two sides to every question." I'm reminded of that every time a political season pushes us into the grip of two dangerously polarized political parties. It seems better to recognize that there are at least 360 sides to every question worth asking and 360 approaches to every problem worth solving. Finding the right approach to homelessness isn't a matter of voting one policy up or down, but of considering the stories of people who live on the streets of a particular city—the challenges of its weather patterns, the dangers of its public health hazards, and the accessibility and scope of its social services. And beyond that, considering the local tax base, the involvement of churches and other places of worship, the mayor's priorities, and so on. One important factor in finding a solution to a problem is the imagination of those invested in the process.

My favorite part of group process is brainstorming—at its best, an exuberant eruption of ideas, some wild, some plausible, some amusing, some brilliant, all unedited and all welcome. Someone pulls out butcher paper or projects a blank screen, and a list begins. As it gets longer, one idea leads to another. Possibilities abound.

An important ground rule in this process is imagining what might be done if money were no object. Or if you could have it all your own way. Or if the naysayers weren't waiting to quash your idea as soon as it gained traction. Ideas and the enthusiasm that fuels them are like tender shoots; they can easily be buried again, or choked out. To give them imaginative space (and soil and air and time) is to allow them to grow roots and become sturdy enough to survive critical scrutiny while they're pruned or transplanted or grafted.

Articulation is a living process; it's what happens to a fetus in the womb as limbs and extremities grow. It's adding defining detail, turning abstractions that lead nowhere into plans that provide direction. When you make a list of possibilities, you articulate a vague idea that grows increasingly specific: "Let's do something" becomes "Let's form an action group" and then "Let's set these priorities for the coming year" and then "Let's fund the plan by hosting a dinner" and then "Let's identify and invite fifty people likely to want to help." And so it goes. As particulars emerge, possibilities expand and take shape and, as they do so, tend to energize everyone involved.

"Never doubt that a small group of thoughtful, committed citizens can change the world," Margaret Mead wrote; "indeed, it's the only thing that ever has." Small groups of thoughtful, committed citizens look at problems, make long lists of possible solutions, winnow those lists, rearrange them, pick action items, and set out. So choose your issue and a few adventurous friends and try one of the lists below.

SOME LISTS TO TRY:

Ways we might relieve electronic stress
What to do with five whole minutes
One project that might improve local schools
Ways to protect kids from sugar
What a local barter system might look like

To identify complicating factors

Very few ventures, I've found, trace a straight line from point A to point B. In the course of any journey, digressions and distractions and obstacles and uncertainties take us one step forward and two back—or a few to the side. Somewhere in early adulthood I learned that there are two reliable answers to most questions people tend to ask: "It depends" and "It's complicated." They're not just evasions—though they can be. Whatever judgment call you need to make or explanation you're called upon to give, more often than not, it *does* depend, and it *is* complicated.

But neither of those answers is sufficient. When we give them, it's good to clarify—for ourselves, at least, if not for those asking the question (since it may be none of their business)—what the decision or judgment call *does* depend on and what the complicating factors *are* that make a change of course or behavior or mind still seem like a good idea. We all have people in our lives who want and deserve to understand why we make the choices we do. And we also have people to whom we are accountable, and we need to find ways to give an account. Recently some of those people asked me some questions to which I felt impelled to reply, "It's complicated":

47

Why did you two decide to move again so soon?

Why did you decide not to continue attending the
group meetings?

Why did you interrupt that promising project to start
another one?

Why don't you call more often? Come see me? Talk
about your work?

You get the idea. Almost any "why" question goes down a winding, branching path that leads through the bright, fenced plots of rationality into the thickets and forests of the psyche and personal history. You may not want to go there; you may somewhere encounter the ancient warning they used to inscribe at the edges of maps of the known world: "Here be dragons."

But if you do go there, armed with a long piece of paper, a pen, and a brave desire for self-knowledge, you might find that listing the complicating factors is revealing and helpful. Whatever the question, what complicates the answer may be worth discovering. You don't always know what the complexities are until you begin to list them. (Let me remind you of another lovely thing about lists: If you keep going, you almost always find yourself adding an item you hadn't anticipated.)

Ashleigh Brilliant, whose quippy postcards used to hang in my office for practical inspiration, published one that featured a puzzled-looking fellow with this caption:

"It's all very simple. Or it's all very complicated. Or neither. Or both." I'd guess both. At the heart of what gets complicated—through the thickets and forests and past the pitfalls and dragons—lie some simple truths.

They have to do with what we want, what we fear, what we value, what we want to protect. We may "simply" want to be happy and at peace. We may "simply" fear pain. We may "simply" value our families or our faith or our honest relationships. We may "simply" want to protect the earth. But all those quotation marks are there because, as writer Ellen Goodman once put it, "The bottom line is always 'It's not that simple.'"

We all know people whose particular grace is a simplicity of spirit or expression that offers welcome without judgment, discretion without evasion, and a quality of intelligence that has nothing to do with credentials. Some I have known and admired are fully capable of grasping complexity and ambiguity, but somehow manage to come "back to center" with ease and grace and steady trust that the center holds.

In my efforts to cultivate that quality, I have found that, paradoxically, lists of complicating factors lead me back to certainties that do hold in the midst of all that winds and twists and entangles. So I recommend the journey. The following lists might provide points of departure:

SOME LISTS TO TRY:

Why I hung on so long
Why I didn't tell anyone
Why I keep it secret
Why I'm postponing what I so clearly want
Why I changed my mind about money

TO MAP THE MIDDLE GROUND

We live in a culture that tends to polarize. Republican or Democrat. North or South. New York or L.A. True or False. Male or Female. Black or white. Rich or poor. Educated or ignorant. Awesome or awful. Normal or abnormal. Healthy or sick. What works, what doesn't. This tendency seems more marked in the U.S. than in some cultures where nuance is both tolerated and required.

A lot goes on between "either" and "or." Sometimes that territory is hard to navigate because it hasn't been mapped, sometimes because we're afraid it's full of landmines or quicksand. But once we venture into it, even a little way, we may find that the middle ground offers not only respite from dithering and debate, but also places where Wisdom dwells.

A good list can get us there. Even though, ultimately, we either change jobs or we don't, and even if at the moment we find ourselves hovering between the job we have and the job we've been offered, it's good to consider the options that lie in the middle ground: applying for a different job; accepting the offered job on slightly different terms; postponing departure for six months; redesigning the job we have in order to stay in it more happily.

When we are called on in troubled seasons of public life to declare our affiliations and positions more frequently and publicly, to vote, to speak, to join groups, to instruct children about the ways of a turbulent world, we will find ourselves needing to enumerate often and carefully the mitigating, modifying factors that shape our position on school curricula or immigration policy, or whether to fund a new sports arena or open mid-town space for a public garden. We live, always, among those with whom we disagree. We need to meet them in the middle, and not necessarily with weapons.

As I get older, my heroes, more than those who "hold tight" and who doggedly "hold fast" to predetermined positions, are those thoughtful souls who know how to negotiate patiently enough to find a shared middle ground. They are capable of civility and choose it over a clash of wits. They know where they can afford to compromise without sacrificing what matters most to any of the parties present. And they know their "talking points"—how to list, briefly and clearly, what brought them to the place between "yes" and "no" that seemed most livable. And, though capable of vigorous debate, they can get there without bitter dispute.

But this doesn't mean that extreme measures or positions aren't sometimes called for and appropriate—only that it might generally be better if they were not the first resort. We need people—and sometimes need to be people—who are willing to go to extremes. But we should also hope to be among those people who can find their way around the middle ground, not mistaking negotiated peace for complicity, or compromise for capitulation, but recognizing what rich territory may be found there, just ready for planting. Some of the lists below might—who knows?—help map the middle ground.

SOME LISTS TO TRY:

Positions I can afford to modify
Possible peace offerings
What lies between a new car and no new car
What might be discovered between right wing
and left wing
Hills I don't want to die on

TO EXPLORE IMPLICATIONS

None of us can see very far down the road, though there are always those who deal in predictions—real prophets, self-appointed prophets, and gamblers who run on calculated risk. I certainly believe that there are real prophets who, in wisdom, humility, and deep attentiveness, receive a word from God for the rest of us, and that the word is often predictive and often includes a warning. I've also come to believe that the gift of prophecy is imparted with a capacity and a willingness to see the implications of present actions: if we keep disobeying God, abusing power, and cheating the poor, it will not go well with us.

I've found a good exercise to make writing and conversation more engaging and substantive. Take a fact or statistic (e.g., "39 percent of California residents are Latinos" or "There are more than 232,000 fast-food restaurants in the U.S.") and consider one of two questions: (1) If that's true, what else is likely to be true?; or (2) If that's true, what else might we need to know to understand the implications of that fact? This exercise helps move us from recitation of facts or abstract opinionating toward reflection on the implications of the facts at hand.

Most facts have implications, just as most acts have consequences, and it's a good exercise to pause over them—and list them—to give our opinions deeper roots. Facts (and, from some quarters, fake facts) come at us thick and fast in public media that are often better at disseminating information than inviting real reflection on it. It takes ten minutes to give the headlines. But a good news program requires a deeper gaze at what those headlines mean, imply, affect, and change.

People who work in medicine, law, psychotherapy, meteorology, engineering, and a good many other professions are carefully trained to find paths from facts to implications. What a symptom means, how to read the evidence, what patterns in an oft-rehearsed narrative may provide a key that unlocks the prison of chronic depression, how changing weather patterns may affect the earth, how a change of material may affect durability—all are examples of those paths. All of these kinds of work rely on lists— checklists, lists of daily medications and their side effects, lists of criteria that keep labels like "organic" meaningful. Lists are a first step toward valid and useful interpretation.

Many of my mornings begin with a conversation in semi-darkness with a spouse who happens to be gifted at dream interpretation. He helps me reflect on possible implications of a dream in such a way as to open up new avenues of self-understanding or direction in decision-making or insight into relationship. In his book *Dream Work*, Jeremy Taylor reminds us that "an astonishingly large number of the cultural ideas and scientific innovations which have shaped our contemporary world were born first as inspirations in dreams. . . ." He also suggests that getting the most guidance or insight from a dream begins with a simple inventory of elements: what objects, persons, spaces, colors, and situations do you remember? Each of them can provide a starting point for reflection.

"Articulating implications" may be just another term for "thinking." It matters that we not lose the habit of thinking things through. Particularly in a culture that encourages many forms of passivity, maintaining the habit of thought requires intention and deliberate exercise. Below are a few facts (culled from what I believe are fairly reliable Internet sources) whose implications might be revealing if you take the time to list them.

SOME LISTS TO TRY:

It takes 1.39 liters of water to produce 1 liter
of bottled water
Refined sugar is more addictive than cocaine
Americans between 8 and 18 average 53 hours a week
on electronic devices
Bees are essential to the human food supply
Drumming helps relieve stress

TO CONNECT THE DOTS

A useful term I picked up from Rebecca Goldstein's engrossing novel *The Mind-Body Problem* is "mattering map." Over time, her protagonist realizes, the mattering map shifts: new relationships resituate old ones; a once-close relative may be consigned to the margins following an outbreak of predictable discord or an uncomfortable Thanksgiving dinner; and what we take to be our guiding principles may reorganize themselves as life gets messier.

We are connected to each other, to the natural and material world around us, and to the ideas we encounter by a vast web of connections. Though, according to a popular theory, we can connect anything to anything else in the world by about "six degrees of separation." Or, to put it another way, any one of us is about six handshakes away from our favorite celebrity or Nobel Prize winner.

In his remarkable and unsettling documentary *A Good American,* Friedrich Moser tells the story of NSA computer scientist William Binney, who invented a surveillance device that could pick up any electronic signal on earth and trace the connections between any two people using electronic devices, while preserving constitutional privacy standards for content. It's actually the story of how that technology was dismantled and its creators disempowered. But my purpose in mentioning it is that Binney and his team took on the daunting task in simple faith that you could, in fact, connect anything with anything because everything is connected.

It's a simple idea—that everything is connected—but one with profound implications. If it's true, I can't entirely separate myself and my story and my welfare and my interests from yours. And what happens to the disappearing species or the rainforests is also happening to me, perhaps less remotely than I'd like to think.

So here's an experiment. Choose any two public issues, but two that seem quite distant from each other, and consider how they're connected. An example might be traffic congestion in Los Angeles and schooling for girls in Afghanistan. One might connect the dots by several different routes. I might be a node in the web of connection: I have some relationship to traffic in L.A., having grown up there, and to girls' schooling, having taught at both a girls' high school and a women's college. The consciousness of the "I" who is doing the connecting may also be a crucial node in the web of connection. Or, the two might be quite objectively connected through market forces, resource distribution, or competing cultural ideologies with long histories of intersection through warfare.

You see what a good game night might be made of this (if you have enough snacks, an Internet connection, and friends with the requisite curiosity). But it's more than that. Connecting the dots helps us stay connected. And staying connected lies at the heart of human community and survival. The instruction reiterated in every wisdom tradition to love our neighbors as ourselves may be more than an admonition to kindness; it may have to do with the fact that our well-being, our growth and happiness and life itself, may depend on our neighbor in ways we can't fully imagine. To foster that love, it can be helpful to "count the ways."

SOME LISTS TO TRY:

Ways I personally depend on the rainforests
What connects me to the people in the local nursing home
What it means to say that children belong to all of us
Why I might need to know what high schools pay for athletic programs
Why it matters who manufactured my sofa

TO GET TO YOUR LEARNING EDGE

Lists go on and on. As long as you let them. Somehow, it seems, there's always more. There are more reasons to shore up your choice, more facets to the problem you're facing, more mysteries to explore in the life of faith, more people to invite, encourage, pray for, respond to, or perhaps avoid. There are more lines to add when you're "counting the ways" you love the beloved. There are more household repairs since the last time you looked.

When I've had students work together to make a list of, say, features of Faulkner's writing or learning moments in *King Lear*, I urge them to continue adding until they get just beyond the point where they think they've said all they have to say.

Just beyond is where the surprises lie. You find yourself adding an insight you didn't know you had in you. Or you find yourself considering how the opposite of an earlier point is also true. Or you begin to think metaphorically. Or your consideration rises to a different level, and the whole list looks different from a new altitude.

Writing lists with others is always a learning event— and I use the term "always" advisedly. If, in a brainstorming session, someone proposes that we make a list of funding sources for a project, that list will always include organizations I haven't heard of or techniques for crowdsourcing I'm way too low-tech to know. If we're listing possible approaches to disciplinary problems on campus, someone from the counseling center or from the physical plant where they deal with the consequences of vandalism will bring a point of view I wouldn't have considered.

I once made a list with a friend of issues that arise in

even the healthiest relationships with adult children, and we both surprised ourselves at how much emerged from that common effort that neither of us likely would have come to on our own.

Years ago I was part of a team of teachers who taught sections of an experimental first-year history course called "From Athens to New York." Rather than studying a long, linear march through history, we were to choose six cities, beginning with ancient Athens and ending with contemporary New York. We were to consider what forces were at work to shape the city's cultural life, bring on or solve problems like epidemics or post-war reconstruction, or feeding and educating the populace. It was an exciting opportunity to take a new look at what used be called "Western Civ" or, more recently, "World Civ"—shorthand for a brief, presumptuous, and inadequate overview of how and where everything has happened. I mention it here because in order to make the task manageable, I made (big surprise!) lists for the students. "Fifteen facts about Johannesburg in the 1990s." "Fifteen facts about London during the Great Plague." And so on. The class spent the first day of studying a new city simply considering each item on the list and its implications.

Whatever benefit the students derived from this exercise, I learned a great deal. Simply selecting items to go on the list was a rich experience of winnowing. And then thinking about the implications of each fact (If this is true, what else is likely to be true? If this is true, what else might we need to know to understand why it's true?)—that took as much time as we were willing to give it. Learning a little provided incentives to look up and learn a little more. (Did you know, for instance, that one-third to one-half of London's residents died during the plague of 1665? Is your interest in epidemics now piqued anew?)

In the interest of such invigoration, try a few of the lists below and see what new learning they lead to.

SOME LISTS TO TRY:

*Fifteen (or more) facts about my
grandmother's early life
Biblical texts I find hard to interpret
Musical [or other field of your choice] terms I'd like
to understand
Why read [a favorite author]—or the daily news
or South Indian novels
What I need to know to be a better gardener*

To notice what you might have missed

Ezra Pound's basic instruction to the poets he worked with was to "make it new"—make language new, make the poetic line work to new purposes, make of poetry a new instrument of awareness. Closely related to lists that take you to your learning edge are lists that take you back to what is deeply familiar and help you "make it new."

If I were to make a list of reasons I love my very familiar husband—say, for Valentine's Day (and that would be rather nice of me, now that I think of it)—I would certainly start with observations about his scintillating conversation, his love of Russian novels and wordplay, his sturdy faith and spiritual depth, his musicality, his laugh. The mere act of listing those things reinvigorates a love that is steady as a heartbeat, yet renewed by such reminders. But as the list goes on, if I let it, I begin to realize things about him that bear more notice than I generally give them: how his hair glistens now that it's turning white; how his musical choices are shifting; how he quietly copes with pain; how he loves rich reds when he paints. Each small observation holds new information about this very familiar person.

Familiar places are similarly worth revisiting. I have long loved Thoreau's wry critique of people who undertook the "grand tour" of Europe when there was so much to see at home. "I have traveled a great deal in Concord," he

62

wrote, which is how, by looking longer and naming what he saw, he came to know the familiar lanes and woods better than any of the townspeople. To take an unaccustomed half-hour to wander slowly through our own back yards might yield gratifying surprises: new buds on a bush, a bird's nest, a place where crabgrass hasn't grown back, a picturesque composition of fallen leaves worth a photograph.

We miss things about our children, our neighbors, even our own bodies. Looking again fosters love as it alerts us to changes and awakens us to new possibilities and introduces fresh avenues of conversation with those we face every night across the dinner table. Below are a few old places to look for what's new.

SOME LISTS TO TRY:

How her face is changing
What's new in the garden
What I hadn't noticed about my nephew
What lies between the lines
Quiet corners where things have been happening

To experience deep attention

A sign that hung on the wall above my desk during my dissertation year has come to mind often since then when I embark on a project: "Attention—deep, sustained, undeviating—is in itself an experience of a very high order." The musician Roberto Gerhard was credited with it, though I don't know on what occasion he said it. But I am thankful to him for putting it just this way. I want just that kind of experience: deep, sustained, undeviating. Sometimes, on quiet, lovely, uninterrupted mornings, I get that gift and am greatly blessed.

Poet Sandra Gilbert calls poems "acts of attention." The way Mary Oliver teaches us to see vultures, the way Gerard Manley Hopkins shows us the world in its "Pied Beauty," the way Yeats foresees the forces of darkness like a gathering cloud over the twentieth century—all bring us to new and sometimes breathtaking moments of attention.

List-making may often be a lighthearted activity, but it requires and elicits attention that can sometimes, without our expecting it, become "deep, sustained, undeviating." As you pause over the items already listed, pen hovering, your mind may drop into something like dream space or a visionary moment where the focus widens and the concern at hand enlarges to include more than you imagined when you set out. So a prayer list for a grandchild—that he may find in tennis a deep well-being of body and spirit, that he may learn what math has to teach him, that his first tentative venture into love may be gentle—might widen into concerns for his generation: that they may find their way humanely through the electronic jungle they inhabit, that they may foster sustainable community, that they may reconnect with the earth, and with God, in ways that keep them close to the Source of all life.

That attention "in itself" is an experience worth having suggests that in some way it doesn't altogether matter what the object of attention is. Even the humble to-do list may foster that habit of mind: each moment of a busy day may be redeemed by entering it with attention, intention, and an abiding sense of the deeper purposes you are serving—your family's welfare, good care of your body, or stewardship of your possessions or relationships with those you've been given to love. The circles widen around any focal point of attention, ultimately connecting us with the divine life that is breathed among and in and through us.

That widening may include the life we share with neighbors, co-workers, those who live in our city, share our roads, provide the village for children—awareness of what's happening in schoolyards, of the plight of the invisible poor among us; awareness of how the elders around us are coping, of how churches are changing, of how video games are normalizing violence; awareness of what discoveries are emerging from research centers and how they change the way we live. Attention to any of these recalls our attention to ourselves not only as individuals with personal concerns but as neighbors and citizens and members of a living body.

In the Byzantine rite of the Eastern Orthodox Church, as the Gospel is about to be read, the priest raises the sacred book high above his head and intones the words, "Wisdom! Be attentive!" Most who attend such services are already attentive. But the words summon them to another level of attention; they rise into it as they stand for the reading. A colloquial equivalent might be when a coach uses the term "Listen up!" when talking to his team, somehow suggesting that attention may be directed with particular fierceness or force or gravity or expectancy to what is about to come.

We have that voice within us, and if we attend to it, calling ourselves to attention can become a habit. Now and then a list can help focus that attention in ways that keep us awake.

SOME LISTS TO TRY:

How I recognize summonings
Small things to do with great love
Unspoken needs I'm noticing around me
Where personal and public life meet
When I "find myself"

TO ENJOY COMPLETE PERMISSION

Lists of prohibitions abound: what not to do at the public pool; where not to smoke; who may not enter a patient's room or administer medications; who may not qualify or come to the closed meeting. The roots of law lie in "thou shalt not." And there are sound reasons for this; prohibitions are fences we build to protect the common good. But some of us, if we grew up thinking that moral and spiritual life was defined entirely by prohibition, may need to practice permission.

Some time ago I taught a course called "Contemplative Reading" in which we practiced *lectio divina*—an ancient exercise of reading Scripture slowly, listening for a word or phrase to dwell on—and extended that practice to poetry and other kinds of literature, learning to read more receptively and imaginatively, and to see what gifts we might glean from reading that served our current needs and seekings. It was a satisfying experience for all of us. On the last day of class, when I asked students what particular words or phrases surfaced for them as they recalled the semester, one of the first mentioned was "permission." They had received permission to take the reading personally, permission to lay aside academic protocols for a while and read for spiritual nourishment and even to play with the rules of reading in new ways.

I was gratified by that recognition of how permission opens the heart and the imagination. I grew up with very loving parents who, though not punitive, were also not quick to grant their children permission. They were cautious—as they needed to be—with money, conscious of time constraints, and a little anxious about our moral development. As a result, I still had things to learn about the goodness of permission, and about how much permission lies in the notion that we are, as Scripture says, "free indeed." One of the great gifts my husband brought into our marriage was a habit of generous permission. He is quick to encourage me to identify my wants, even if we can't satisfy them all, go where my imagination takes me, try things out, and give the "shoulds" a rest when it's time to play.

In that spirit, at the beginning of Lent one year, I put together a talk: "Lent: A Time of Permission." Most of us think of Lent as a time of giving something up for the sake of spiritual openness and focus. But I've discovered that reframing the invitation of the season in terms of permission actually brings me closer to its purpose. Here's my list of what Lent gives us:

Permission to seek deeper pleasures rather than mere distractions

Permission to pause rather than hurry onward
Permission to eat well and mindfully
Permission to renew relationship with God and others
Permission to try new experiments with prayer

These might be seen as spiritual practices, but I find that thinking of them as specific permissions opens up the season of Lent as a rich and inviting time of renewal.

And as I claim permission, I also want to practice giving permission where I might be inclined for the wrong reasons to withhold it: to find ways to say yes to grandchildren that will affirm their best interests; to allow my husband a little more uninterrupted time to paint; to make it comfortable for people around me to speak their minds even where we differ. Our freedom as children of a loving God is expressed in the permission we give ourselves and others to live by the Spirit who moves among us and speaks in the secret places of our hearts.

SOME LISTS TO TRY:

Permissions I need to give myself
Where I feel unpermitted
Who needs my permission
Permissions I've found in Scripture
What I can afford to allow, even though it annoys me

Part II

THE WAY OF THE LIST-MAKER

If you've read this far, you've probably been making your own lists for a while, so the remaining reflections and exercises are simply an offering from a fellow list-maker, extended in the hope of encouraging you to keep long sheets of paper handy and make your way down them in due time. Because listing is a life skill. Because lists hold us accountable: they make us more specific, and specificity is a kind of responsibility we need to urge on the political leaders, preachers, and public speakers who fog the airways with abstractions. It takes a certain courage to be specific, because the more specific we are, the more we expose ourselves to objections or obligations. But specificity is also empowering. We can't act with energy or direction if we aren't specific about our intentions. So listing can become an important step in making ourselves more responsible, reflective, attentive, intentional members of our families and communities.

Things to do to the to-do list

Consider the humble to-do list. It's ordinary. It can be a motivator, but more often it's an annoyance. It gives us a daily dose of guilt, if we let it, and tastes a little worse than cod-liver oil. The other day I spoke to a friend who admitted she couldn't remember ever having accomplished everything on her daily to-do list, though she continues (surprisingly) to write them. What she did remember were the many days when she'd done nothing on the list. Nothing.

What's interesting about her story is not the fact that she so seldom does what's on her lists, but that she keeps writing them. One has to assume that, though they're recipes for frustration, they also serve some other purpose. I happen to know that she's a woman who gets a great deal accomplished, so her languishing to-do lists provide no accurate measure of her effectiveness. But they may do one of several other things. They may counterbalance her wild and active imagination and keep her grounded as she responds to the many invitations a day brings. They may help her determine what can be put off for a while. They may enable her to see what things she may not really have to do, after all. Think of the long mental lists Thoreau might have made as he happily hoed his beans and didn't go shopping.

I also write to-do lists which, if I saved them, would provide a rather embarrassing record of things left undone—as one might readily determine by the number of items on Monday's list that show up several days in succession. But sometimes a simple to-do list opens up into a wider range of intentions and hopes. It reveals the things I want to do today, the things I clearly don't want to do (a list that may lead to thoughtful identification of particular resistances), the things I hope to complete this week or month, the things I'd like to do for others, the things I plan to do when I have world enough and time, the things I'd like to learn to do, the things I'm hoping to persuade my long-suffering spouse to do with me, and the things I want to do before I die.

That last is an invigorating list to revisit periodically. My journey on earth will have an end. And even if I do go on to life in another dimension, I can't take my half-finished projects or unfulfilled travel plans with me. So now and then I wonder about that list. Is a trip to India still on it? And should that move up a few notches, because adapting to plane travel and unfamiliar food is only going to get harder? And have I, in fact, written a health-care directive and a will that will give our children a gift of clarity when the time comes?

In times of political urgency, a to-do list might become an activist's handbook: Call your senators; get to the schoolboard meeting; write an op-ed piece; attend a fundraiser. In times of personal loss, it might be a lifeline, keeping you connected to daily life when grief threatens to overwhelm. Or in times of celebration, it could be a space for imagining ways to make love visible.

You might try letting a simple to-do list become less simple. Or whittle a daunting list down to five things and say why they're the ones that matter. Or make it an invitation to a particular person: things you hope to do with him or her, including notes on how you imagine making those things happen.

Or you could write down one item and pin it to your wall for the day: "Nothing." Doing nothing is very hard for some of us. Taking a real retreat, a real rest, a real Sabbath—that may be the real challenge. That intention is worth inscribing—writing it, if need be, on your lintels and doorposts. Or any of these: Breathe. Open. Rest. Enjoy. Receive. Release. Sleep. Go in peace.

One to-do list I wrote recently came after I drove through a downtown area where homelessness continues to be a visible, heartbreaking problem. Churches and city council members and local food banks and veterans' groups are hard at work finding ways to help, but I felt helpless. So I needed to regroup, rethink, and consider how to redirect my own efforts:

Things to do for the homeless here in town

Show up at church and make sandwiches
Stop and talk a little
Support the local food bank
Find out who's running the shelters and what they need
Buy extra supplies when you go to the drugstore
Make eye contact
Carry an extra blanket to give away when it's cold
Listen to their stories and relay them

OR TRY PLAYING WITH ONE OF THESE:

Things to do when I'm feeling down
Things to do more often with the ones I love
Things to do to improve the world if I can't save it
Things to do with small children
Things to delegate

HOW TO DO ALMOST ANYTHING

Almost every magazine at the supermarket check-out stand features one or more of these kinds of how-tos. How to lose fifty pounds in forty weeks. How to keep your kids off drugs. How to make a company supper in twenty minutes. How to parent a small child. Or a surprisingly large child. Or an adult child. How to be an effective speaker or gardener or organizer. Magazines offering how-tos have proliferated because they sell. And they sell because we're all suckers for simple instructions. We'd love to be able to learn the skills we admire in twelve easy steps. Or seven. Or five.

Of course, that impulse to simplify may come from impatience with the long, slow period of apprenticeship that precedes mastery. I've dismayed many a first-year college student with the unwelcome news that there's no simple formula or recipe for writing well. The "five-paragraph essay" most of them learned in high school is not going to serve their more complex purposes as they age into adulthood. On that note, we embark on a journey I hope some of them are still on, which takes them from one paragraph, essay, article, or memoir to the next in a spirit of discovery and a practice that is new every morning. There are some fairly good all-purpose guidelines for this journey, but no simple how-to list.

Still, writing a how-to list can offer an approach to a skill that gives the beginner a foothold, or even reminds the skilled of some basic principles as they work their way through a practical problem. A written recipe may not guarantee the nuance an experienced chef brings to a dish by knowing when to add a "dash" more of a key spice, but it can help ensure you don't use too much baking soda or bake at too high a temperature. And there's no recipe for good tennis; some of it has to be learned by playing. But a good coach will give you rules of thumb that return to you when you need them in the middle of a match.

Simply making a "how-to" list can help us clarify our own processes, make new possibilities apparent, and sometimes get us through times when we muddle or flail or meander through our own confusions because we haven't slowed down enough to sit with the "how" question and let the answers come.

A FEW HOW-TOS TO TRY:

How to get more out of boring meetings
How to reclaim what's getting lost in the noise and haste
How to spend good time with a person with dementia
How to cope with a steady stream of bad news
How to be a better friend

Playing favorites

Every kid likes to do this. Who among us who has any small children in the family circle hasn't repeatedly—sometimes tediously—asked, "What's your favorite color?" "What's your favorite game?" "What's your favorite dessert?" More to the point, which of us hasn't then listened to a solemn recitation of favorites, judiciously considered and pronounced with complete conviction. When a child tells you "Orange is my favorite color," she may be offering encoded information worth probing with a few questions. "Why orange?" might yield very little good information, since she probably doesn't know. But if you ask, "What orange things do you have in your house?" or "What orange things do you like to eat?" or "Who does orange remind you of?", you might learn a few things about a small person whose psyche is every bit as complex as your own.

My favorite six-year-old isn't the only one who loves the innocent exuberance of Julie Andrews singing "My Favorite Things" to the nightgowned Von Trapp children. That scene reminds all of us (as we settle in once again with popcorn and a little Kleenex to watch *The Sound of Music*) of the joy of playing favorites.

Naming favorites isn't an altogether idle activity, even for adults whose daily to-do lists don't generally make much reference to this humble practice. When I name my favorite foods, I become a little more aware of my eating habits, of emotional attachments to certain "comfort foods" or of those I regard as indulgences or rewards or acquired tastes. I am reminded again that food choices really are consequential. A food inventory can open a door to a deeper awareness of eating habits, and a lot of us could stand to modify those—if not sign up for a program that promotes a complete culinary overhaul.

Naming my favorite books has proven to be not only a valuable autobiographical exercise, but a help in choosing what students might be ready to read. I remember when reading *Little Women* on the platform my grandfather built in our plum tree was my idea of an afternoon of bliss. I remember Tara as vividly as Scarlett O'Hara must have, since I dwelt there for all the shining moments it took to get me through six hundred pages, almost unconscious of the sound of passing traffic and Saturday chores. I remember discovering Thoreau's *Walden* and resolving then and there (and many times since) to simplify my life— and cast a cold eye on convention. I remember reading *Moby-Dick* with deepening reverence in graduate school, though a classmate declared it a "seven-hundred-page joke on the reader." All these memories have helped me as a mother and mentor and teacher and elder when I have had the privilege of guiding the young into places of literary pleasure.

Naming favorites also helps as friends and partners get

to know one another. That my husband knows my favorite poet (still T. S. Eliot, though he has some competitors), my favorite style of clothing (long tunics—can't see why we all don't wear them), my favorite breakfast food (kale smoothie—yum!), and my favorite British actor (Emma Thompson) enables him to please and surprise me on occasion in ways that make us both happy. And that I know his favorites also serves us well. In fact, it seems to me that premarital counseling should allow generous time for crafting lists of favorites to exchange and tuck away for future reference.

Naming favorites is an exercise in self-knowledge, values clarification, and discernment, as well as a valuable part of decision-making. I recommend that it be repeated frequently, for fun if not for profit, preferably with friends and loved ones.

SOME "FAVORITES" LISTS TO PLAY WITH:

Favorite films of the past five years
Favorite political commentators and journalists
Favorite ways to care for my body and well-being
Favorite gifts I've been given
Favorite lines from poems or songs

THE WONDER OF WORD LISTS

Adam, so the story goes, was given the privilege of naming the things of this earth. Naming is still a privilege. Witnessing the delight of a child first learning words for things awakens in all of us, I imagine, a poignant appreciation of what deep pleasure and potential lie in simple utterance. I still admire and envy biologists and botanists and physicists and musicians whose personal vocabularies include so many precise, complex, and beautiful names for things.

Word lists lead us into corners of our language life that may have lain fallow for far too long. The linguists who claim that most average educated adults have a vocabulary of 15,000 to 20,000 words but use fewer than 2,000 of them have a point to make: most of us could be speaking with more nuance, emotional variety, surprise, pleasure, and wit than we do. Word lists allow us to exhume words we buried with our eighth-grade vocabulary lists. If we give ourselves thirty seconds to come up with synonyms for "hurry," for instance, or ways of saying "Be calm," we might notice how one or another of them articulates a particular angle of vision or feeling or triggers a memory worth pondering.

I've often given students in my writing classes this exercise: "You have one minute. Write down all the verbs you can think of for what light does." Starting with the obvious—it shines, illuminates, glows—we very soon start imagining light in other ways: it glistens, scatters, dances. Then we see that it oozes, seeps, bends, breaks, splays. And so on. If we keep going, we may find ourselves looking up "light" and learning a little more about physics and photons, rays and waves. We may end up in what one physicist called "radical amazement."

As a practical exercise, making word lists enriches writing life by focusing closer attention on shades of meaning, training us in greater precision. The difference between *delight* and *gladness*, for instance, may seem slight, but the words have different histories, different tonalities, and different effects. As in the example above, verbs, when properly used, can help us understand processes more accurately, more inclusively, more imaginatively, and more compassionately. I add that last because so many processes in public life are covered over with glib generalities or tired clichés, and need to be looked at with clarity and compassion in order to be changed.

Take *legislate,* a verb that covers a multitude of arduous tasks performed by whole teams of people whose motives and remuneration need to be examined regularly. Or *deal with*, a colloquialism which is commonly used to suggest that measures are being taken to address a problem, but which actually means very little. A list of verbs might offer valuable answers to questions about what it means to "deal with" an awkward situation or a threat or an adversary. They might include words like *confront* or *disarm,* or *diagnose* and *treat,* or *discuss* and *dispatch.* The longer the list, the more likely it becomes that we will arrive at some insight about the nature of action that we hadn't predicted or known we needed.

A variation on the word list is a list of phrases. Phrases often carry evocative power, especially when they're borrowed from poems, sacred texts, songs, hymns, speeches made on historic occasions, or daily life in one's own family culture. It's impossible, I imagine, for any adult American to hear the phrase "with malice toward none" without the sorrow and the pity and the wisdom of Lincoln's Second Inaugural Address coming to mind. Even if one can't recite the whole stately paragraph, the occasion of so much loss and the intention of an anguished leader to forgive and make amends are both concentrated in that phrase.

A list of phrases from hymns can be a useful starting point for reviewing one's faith journey. Mine might begin with "trust and obey"—the title of a hymn my mother sang as a lullaby—and continue with "join with all nature in manifold witness" or "the love which from our birth over and around us lies" and "heart of my own heart, whatever befall." When I move from phrase to phrase, it becomes newly apparent to me what faith has felt like, what curiosities and doubts and consolations have occurred in the course of my wanderings.

Words and phrases are "the things we carry." They are equipment for living. Listing them keeps them available, usable, and sharp as a scalpel for the life-saving work we may be called to.

SOME LISTS TO PLAY WITH:

Shades of red
Antique words that deserve to be retrieved
Words I like just because they're delicious
Phrases from our family culture
What babies do with their bodies

ALLOWING LAMENT

One healthy response to the popular British injunction to "Keep calm and carry on" is to "Rage, rage against the dying of the light." There's something to be said for both coping strategies. Here, let us say a word for the way of lament. Lamentation almost always involves a list of woes or longings or painful confusions. It certainly has biblical endorsement, as well as the weight of literary tradition from the ancient Greeks onward. Aeschylus's words about suffering have lasted these thousands of years because they ring true: "Even in our sleep, / pain which cannot forget / falls drop by drop upon the heart / until, in our own despair, against our will, / comes wisdom through the awful grace of God."

No one knows this better than those who have been enslaved, persecuted, unjustly imprisoned, oppressed, exiled, or witness to atrocities no human should have to bear. A vast literature of lament has emerged from sites of sorrow, one notable and lively example being African-American spirituals and Gospel songs that mingle pain and hope in ways that forestall glib and false comfort. "Nobody knows the trouble I've seen." "Sometimes I feel like a motherless child." "I'm a-rollin' thro' an unfriendly world." These are just a few of the many eloquent lines that remind us of the character, duration, scope, and depth of suffering none of us can afford to forget.

Our own Declaration of Independence is a list of grievances—a form of public declaration that Jefferson and Franklin borrowed from earlier lists of the same kind; the Magna Carta's long list of intentions rests on specific forms of suffering inflicted on the people which, its makers insisted, would no longer be tolerated. A brief search on the Internet turns up a number of documents written in that spirit, springing from religious and secular groups alike—litanies of lament, lists of complaints, outcries and protests and challenges to power abusers. Undoubtedly we need the voices that cry out—long and clear.

In 2012 Joan de Vries posted a "Litany of Lament" that asks plaintively, "How long will mere children become soldiers?" and "How long must women be made into sexual objects?" and "How long before governments rule justly?" In 2015 Rachel Hackenberg posted a similar piece, boldly appealing to God—"Uncover your ears and know your people's anguish"—and then listing psalm-like pleas: "Do not hide yourself from the cries for relief, from the noises of war. . . . Do not hide yourself from the lament across colleges and in the West Bank, from the wailing and the protesting. . . . Do not hide yourself from the tears in Paris and Calais, from the devastation of death. . . . Do not hide yourself from the women in Japan, from the women in Beirut, from the daughters and sisters endangered by the world's agitation."

And in 2016 Mennonite pastor Joanna Shenk wrote a comparable and similarly timely litany of lament that includes a series of lines that begin with "We are outraged," followed by lines beginning "We acknowledge," that focus on our complicity in the evils that outrage us, then lines beginning "We lament" that name sites of violence, and finally lines that begin "We pray." All of these model a process, private or public, that helps guide us through the worst of times.

Clearly lament is more complicated, richer, and more useful than mere fist-shaking or abject wailing. "My face is red with weeping," writes the author of the book of Job, "and on my eyelids is deep darkness." The Psalmist cries, "How long, O Lord? Will you forget me forever? . . . Must I have sorrow in my heart all the day?" The prophet Jeremiah, surveying the suffering of land and people, writes, "I will take up weeping and wailing for the mountains, and a lamentation for the pastures of the wilderness, because they are laid waste." And in Psalm 60 King David counts up the people's sufferings, insisting that God do something soon: you have rejected us, broken our defenses, been angry, made the land to quake, torn it open, made the people see hard things, given us wine to drink that made us stagger.

Psalms, songs, poems, and other lamentations often emerge at moments we might describe as just before dawn. In that darkest time of night, the tipping point that turns us away from despair and toward some glimmering of hope has often been inscribed in lists of sorrows one cannot, and perhaps should not, release without naming them. To look at the whole, sorry lot of our sufferings can be an important step toward release.

Naming empowers not only the sufferer but those who hope to help. Doctors, for instance, need as detailed a list of patients' pains as they can get to do their job well. Therapists' work consists of inviting clients to name their anxieties. As Thomas Hardy memorably wrote, "If way to the better there be, it exacts a full look at the worst."

Those of us who were taught not to complain, to keep a stiff upper lip, to take a certain pride in what we can put up with—we may need to list our laments more than others. To give ourselves that permission may liberate the energy we expend keeping a lid on what needs to be released, or at least seen clearly enough to enable us to devise effective ways of living with what we cannot entirely dispel. Most of us might easily find a place to begin in our most intimate losses. I think of Auden's wrenching poem for a lost beloved with its anguished, angry imperatives: "Stop all the clocks, cut off the telephone, / Prevent the dog from barking . . . silence the pianos . . . pack up the moon and dismantle the sun . . . pour away the ocean. . . ." The enormity of personal grief in this poem has articulated for millions of readers what seems otherwise "unspeakable."

According to Norman O. Brown, "The way out is down and out." If he's right, then lists, like stairways into subterranean places, can take us there, and perhaps help lead us out again.

SOME LISTS TO TRY IN TRYING TIMES:

Things I will miss about her
What weighs on my heart

Cracks where the light gets in
What I see when I descend to the depths
Losses that have changed me

HOW A LIST BECOMES A POEM

Some years ago I wrote a list in a moment of personal reflection that I then sent to *Weavings*, a journal of Christian spirituality that occasionally printed one-page pieces. After that list was published a few months later, I was surprised to receive a number of very kind replies from readers who said my "poem" had meant a lot to them. Their responses were touching; the surprise lay in the fact that they read the list as a poem. I do write poetry on occasion—mostly when I can't beat a graceful retreat into prose—but I hadn't thought of the list as a poem.

As a longtime teacher of poetry, I should have connected those dots.

Many poems begin as lists—or are lists. Barbara Ras's delightful poem "You Can't Have It All," while it repeats that withering reminder several times, consists otherwise of a long list of what, nevertheless, you *can* have, including "the fig tree and its fat leaves like clown hands," "the touch of a single eleven-year-old finger / on your cheek, waking you at one a.m. to say the hamster is back," "the purr of the cat and the soulful look / of the black dog . . . ." Carole Satyamurti's poem "I Shall Paint My Nails Red" offers a list of startling reasons for doing so, among which are "because a bit of color is a public service," "because I will look like a survivor," and "because my daughter will say ugh."

Among the many poems that elevate lists into the annals of "serious" literature are many of Walt Whitman's, whose "catalogues" of types of people, states of feeling, and forms of human activity continue for more pages than most undergraduates care to read. I would add to that list Christopher Smart's "Jubilate Agno," which (some think inexplicably) includes dozens of lines beginning with "Let" that decree how particular parties shall rejoice. And, for the general edification of readers insufficiently aware of earthy, biological processes, I would also add A. R. Ammons's "Shit List: Omnium-gatherum of Diversity into Unity," which gleefully lists, with frequent parenthetical comments, the various kinds of animal shit that make up the soil we live by.

But not all lists are poems. Lists become poems when poetic devices come into play, sometimes without the list writer's recognizing at first that the list is growing up to be a poem. One line offers a metaphor. Another establishes a rhythm that bears repetition. Or alliteration happens and then happens again. Or one line will break into the next with an enjambement that wasn't foreseen, but works to a pleasing effect. As lines emerge, they lead in a direction the list-writer hadn't fully foreseen.

And then, when it's clear that the list is acting like a poem, it begs for pruning the way a healthy tree does: you see where a little more light might come through. You also see how a phrase or image might serve a double purpose, how varying line lengths might give the whole a shape, like the curve notes travel in a line of music. And musicality begins to matter a bit more than you had anticipated. As all this happens, you may find your attention moving from meaning to sound to the feelings each line evokes as the layering of lines achieves something greater than the sum of its parts. My best advice for fellow list-makers at this point is to let it happen. Watch it happen. Witness your own process as you tinker and tweak and step back to consider the total effect. And, as with most art, it's good to stop just a little before you think you've said everything.

While many list poems are fairly simple, playful exercises in association, some serve more solemn purposes: as each item is added, awareness is heightened or sorrow deepened or empathy widened. Kevin Taylor's "No Justice on Stolen Land," for instance, which simply lists places where quiet, persistent protest has been registered against a long legacy of systemic abuse, connects sites of resistance into a constellation a continent wide:

Along Victoria Inner Harbour
Behind the granite wall
Next to Capt. James Cook's effigy in bronze
Next to bold bronze plaques of white-worlders-
    come-by-water
Across from *The Empress*
In front of the Assembly of Other Nations
Under an iron bench
Scratched in concrete—
No justice on stolen land.

One of its various poetic effects is the recurring focus on earthy substances—water, granite, bronze, iron, concrete, and soil itself—that traces a kind of geological history more natural than nationhood, that outlives all claims and, as most native peoples believe, defies "ownership." Among the sound effects that unite the lines is a smooth assonance—opening vowels that connect lines fluidly like water: *along, inner, effigy, Empress, Assembly, iron*. Speaking them requires a particular movement at the back of the throat, a momentary but palpable pause that slows the progress of thought. This is important because the work of a good poem is to postpone the too-rapid drift from sensation to feeling to idea to abstraction. A poet's work is to call our attention to the dew on the grass blade before it evaporates altogether—the moment, the single act, the half-hidden inscription, the fleeting feeling, and, as Wallace Stevens would remind us, what happens "just after."

Not all lists become poems, or need to. But if one wants to, it's good to invite the good angels of list-making to alight, and to accept the gift they bring. Here are some possibilities to play with. They may just offer occasions for other kinds of experimentation. Then again, they may want to be poems—and if they do, let them.

SOME LISTS THAT MAY WANT TO BE POEMS:

What she brought with her into the room
Moments I had almost forgotten
What I really needed
Small things that have mattered
What I must be willing to witness

HOW A LIST BECOMES A PRAYER

I know a number of faithful people who keep prayer lists for daily use, paying generous attention to others' particular needs, sometimes asking what to pray for so that they might focus the energy of their prayers like a laser beam directly on what needs to be healed or clarified or resolved. One of them asked me once, months after I had mentioned a concern to her, whether it had been resolved and if she might take it off her list for the time being. I was both startled and touched by her fidelity to the small, significant task of praying for me in such a quietly sustained way.

Prayer lists can easily become rote, of course. Children often learn to pray for others by means of the nightly recitation of family folk: "God bless Mommy and Daddy and Johnny and Susie (if she stops being mean) and Biscuit the dog and Sinbad the cat and all the goldfish." Such prayers, sweet as they can be, stagnate if the lists aren't refined and focused and widened and rooted in humble recognition that all of us need, periodically, to ask again, "Lord, teach us to pray."

But the listing impulse is good because it keeps our prayers from falling into a deepening groove of self-preoccupation, and makes us mindful of the needs around us. If we think concentrically about those needs, the list might widen from self to family to school and church, to the local streets to the wild spaces nearby (and all their struggling creatures) to state and nation, to the planet we share and the condition of its atmosphere and oceans. That's a large agenda, to be sure, but it focuses prayer energy on every dimension of life on earth and keeps us aware of ourselves as pilgrims and sojourners, partners and parents, neighbors and strangers, and sometimes the only passerby available to respond to the call of the moment.

A prayer list can deepen and sharpen our focus as well as widen it. When I pray for my granddaughter, for her life and learning in school, for her health and happiness, I may also find on my list of her needs some things that open doors to further reflection on what it may be like to be a girl-child of six in this culture and this place—what pressures she feels to grow up too soon, what kinds of decisions her parents have to keep making about all she's exposed to when she walks out the door. I become aware of how early girls are induced to think of themselves in sexualized terms, how vulnerable they are to subtle, if not overt, forms of abuse, how easily their spontaneity can be crushed by meanness, and how their confidence may need to be fostered by adults who take them seriously.

A mental list of moments I have witnessed (or one written down for the purpose) can keep my thoughts about this child connected to my heartfelt experience of who she is: watching her do an unplanned dance in an empty room; noticing how fiercely she concentrates when she's reading a story to herself; appreciating the care with which she cracks an egg and stirs a bowl of batter; understanding, when her face quiets and her gaze strays, how already she has learned to contain small sorrows and process them in the secret places of her own being. All these images help me pray for Hannah. I commend to you a list of re-membered moments as a point of departure for deepening prayer. Or any of the ones below.

LISTS THAT MIGHT PUSH OUT
THE EDGES OF PRAYER LIFE:

Policymakers under pressure
What leaders are carrying
What help may be needed now
What needs to be clarified
What comfort might look like

A LONG SECOND LOOK

Some lists open new avenues of exploration, offer new insights, send us off to look things up and find things out. Some, on the other hand, invite us to revisit the familiar and reconsider, re-evaluate, reframe, or revise. They show us things we didn't know we knew—things that have been there all the time. Most lists, like most poems, establish a lively, creative tension between old and new, obvious and oblique, what we have accepted or integrated and what we have excluded or avoided. Valuable learning moments may occur when we write lists for the express purpose of looking again.

For years I imagined teaching a course that, alas, has thus far remained untaught. In it my students and I would read together only books everyone had already read at least once. The class was to be called "A Second Look at Certain Books." The goal would be to notice what one notices the second time around, when the plot is known, and the pace and the general point. The second (or fifth or ninth) time through a book or museum or symphony or forest, one not only recognizes what one missed the first time, but discovers new layers or shades of meaning in what one "got." So one not only adds new landmarks to the map but connects the dots differently. And that's when new constellations appear.

I remember the long second look I took at the story of my dad's life as I knew it when I was preparing a talk for his funeral. I was stricken to realize how much I didn't know about the man who had brought us kids up on his war stories, stories of stowing away on a ship, selling newspapers on street corners, writing for a movie magazine, romancing our mother from half a world and half a lifetime away. I suddenly realized how much he hadn't told: gaps in the rich fabric of his stories became painfully evident. There were things I would never know. Recognizing that rearranged what I thought I did know. I began to see his life story in new ways.

Similar kinds of reconsideration come when we reread beloved books. Our sympathies shift as we bring our own life lessons to bear on characters who once seemed heroic and now seem rash, or who once seemed appealingly demure and now seem timid. A favorite biblical parable opens a different point of entry: we read the prodigal son's story once again, but give more thought to the father's predicament, or the elder brother's.

A list of what we see when we look again can bring those new insights into sharper focus. Reconsidering failures in light of "What I learned," for instance, can open new avenues of humility, consolation, and encouragement. Remembering defining losses in terms of "What came in the wake of loss" might become more than a simple exercise in counting your blessings, as it complicates the category of "loss" in new ways. Or a long, fresh look at a frustrating teen might open opportunities for tenderness and even a little humor as you consider "What's beyond the black lipstick."

On a larger scale, we might consider a slow reassessment of what we were taught about history in light of our more adult understanding of (or confusion about) political life and leadership. Taking the measure of "What I know now" can be both revealing and convicting. In that same spirit, one might explore "What I know now" about reading the Bible, or raising children, or the costs of travel, or the food on the table, or the river one lives by. These would be good lists to make and tuck away, then revisit in five years with a sharp new pencil and a sharp new frame of mind.

Below are some other lists that might help us open our eyes or minds or hearts to something we haven't sufficiently reconsidered.

RECONSIDERATIONS TO CONSIDER:

Things I've found just behind the obvious
Things Mom might have said
What my civics teacher seems to have left out
Missed opportunities to be reclaimed
Corrections for the record: Things to explain at my funeral

MEMENTO MORI

Having just made mention of funerals and the backward glance, this piece might seem redundant, but the specific matter of commemoration, a task that often falls to a family member in a time of loss or to a leader on a public anniversary, poses a challenge: how to claim the occasion for our present purposes rather than capitulating to the downward pull of nostalgia and sentimentality.

Recently I gave myself seventy-five minutes of pure pleasure watching Joan Baez and other singers perform for her seventy-fifth birthday celebration. For some of us, the participants were like a parade of old friends: David Crosby, Emmylou Harris, Mavis Staples, Paul Simon, Judy Collins, Jackson Browne, and others. For those of us of a certain age, their voices evoked an invigorating period in public life. They sang to sustain us in the midst of a long, painful, shameful war. They sang to support civil rights. They sang us through the complexities of coming of age while political sands shifted and old myths melted in the fires of social reform. As the camera panned the New York audience, the prevalence of baby boomers was evident—all of them visibly enjoying a chance to hear and sing old songs in a new moment. But it was, clearly and intentionally, a new moment. Joan and the others made sure it wasn't an idle trip down memory lane, but an occasion still fierce with awareness, committed to harmony, both literal and figurative, and unabashedly candid about once again, in a new sense, coming of age.

They did sing old songs, but in new ways, some of them more gently, some more playfully, some pointedly refocused on current public concerns. Because remembering doesn't mean returning so much as reassembling—

literally piecing together what has been dismembered by the drift of time, generally in new patterns, since, as poet Chana Bloch puts it, "the past keeps changing."

As a deliberate act of remembering, commemoration can serve a variety of purposes. A list of achievements in an obituary written for a company publication may allow workers and management to reconsider their purposes together. A list of loving moments in a mother's life can do far more than abstract words like *kind* and *cheerful* and *faithful* to convey the quality of her love in ways that will honor her and inspire those who lost her. A list of names like those engraved on the Vietnam memorial in Washington reminds us that each person who died in that horrifying war had a family—might have been named for an uncle, must have had Irish ancestors, or Italian, or African, very likely left behind loved ones who watched him or her grow—and had a story. A short one.

Since many commemorations, even in times of loss, are also celebrations, the good ones pay rich homage to what there is to celebrate: courage, fidelity, skill, and generosity, to be sure, but it is in specifics that we come to feel and understand each of those things. Listing the generous things someone has done gives life to what otherwise remains a pious abstraction, and may complicate it in important ways. It could, for example, be an act of generosity for a teacher to make an angry kid stay in the classroom at lunchtime if she gives up her own break and stays with him to see him through a bad moment. Or generosity could come as silence that makes room for someone else in conversation.

Celebrations of the usual things we commemorate can always be enhanced by the long look a list requires. Walt Whitman knew this when he began his long poem "Song of Myself," much of it an elaborate list, with the brash and joyful words, "I celebrate myself and sing myself." When a baby is born, a list of the blessings she is born into can strengthen hope and deepen joy in a sometimes scary moment. When a couple gets married, the list of the friends in the guest book can remind them of how they are held and sustained in a web of community. At graduation, a list of "Things I've learned" or "What I'd like to know now" can keep the occasion grounded in something deeper than a class trip to Disneyland.

The key to commemoration is specifics. See how specific you can be in one or more of the lists below.

REMEMBERINGS:

What I remember about my aunt
What seventh grade felt like
What war looks like
Those who made the difference
How we knew he was called to be a coach

SWITCHING LENSES

A list can be a valuable exercise in reframing, which means seeing a situation in new terms. To get a new angle of vision, it helps to itemize those terms. To see a loss as an opportunity, for instance, isn't easy when you're in the midst of it, but simply naming the opportunities it opens up, or might open up, can help you find a way through disappointment and anxiety. Such a list might be something like "What I might learn about myself now" or "What I get to try out" or "What remains."

Reframing often requires courage. The terms in which we see most things that matter are established by convention, family custom, newspapers, textbooks, and the expectations of the people around us. To tell the narrative of U.S. history not as a triumphant and glorious conquest of "virgin" land, but as a complicated story of empire built at the expense of lives and species may not be appropriate for fifth-graders, but might, a little later, help prevent dangerous oversimplifications. There's a dark side to every story, and a time to acknowledge it.

Of course, not all reframing takes us to the dark side. To see a difficult family member not in terms of how his behavior affects you but in terms of the needs behind that behavior can infuse painful memories or encounters with a measure of compassion. Or to see one's own regrets as perhaps necessary losses, lessons, exercises in humility, or stations on the way to wisdom can soften self-judgment, help us accept what has been, and live a little more freely in the present. Imagine, for instance, a litany of release—a ritual of dropping the regrets you carry one by one into a deep, clear pool of divine forgiveness where they will be dissolved. It could be as simple as a list naming the regrets: "Things I didn't do for my dying father" or "Unkept promises" or "What I would do now." Such a list could also be elaborated into an actual litany, each line ending with "I ask and receive forgiveness": "For the preoccupation that kept me from paying attention when my child was in pain . . . I ask and receive forgiveness."

On a lighter note, a list that deliberately reframes may be purely playful. And play matters immensely; it's a way of stepping into life with full consent and joyful authority. It keeps the heart limber and open. So, for instance, try overturning a tired platitude and see what happens. The experiment might just allow you to embrace a paradox that prevents moral rigidity. What if a little rudeness is exactly what the occasion calls for? How might you and others benefit if you simply gave up a particular task? What if it's time to enjoy spending that "penny saved" or to allow yourself to go late to bed and be late to rise? What might be worth doing even if you'll never do it well enough to go public?

Early in his retirement from full-time work, my husband took to painting (speaking of the courage to embark on inexpert endeavors) and gradually produced some remarkable pieces that now enliven our walls. One of the earliest showed a series of intersecting frames against a background of color—as though they were hanging in space. They were startling, evocative, and sometimes, as I gazed at them, slightly disturbing in the way they reminded me of how many intersecting frames and structures we navigate on our journeys toward true consciousness, and how we dwell among borders and boundaries, forgetting how free we were made to be. But his frames seemed to be hanging in space like a Calder mobile, as though a puff of wind might move them all into new configurations. And so it might. As the old King James Bible puts it, the Spirit "bloweth where it listeth," and when it blows, the landscapes of our lives may be radically reframed.

Below are a few titles for lists that might reframe what is "normal" or threatening or tedious and make it new.

REFRAMINGS:

Valuable distractions
What to neglect

What doesn't matter as much as I thought
When pieties don't play well
When to harden my heart

BETTER THAN A PUNCHING BAG

Lists of grievances serve many purposes. One is to focus, funnel, and eventually defuse anger. You have to put anger somewhere while you wait for it to dissipate, die, be dispelled by prayer or meditation, fade into mild annoyance, or find its way into vigorous, rational, kindly conversation. Contrary to certain popular doctrines, it doesn't always help to "let anger out," especially if "letting it out" means spewing it into a room where other people are likely to breathe in its toxicity. But a very specific list that identifies and clarifies the pain or the disappointment or the fear that lies behind the anger can sometimes pave a pathway to peace. The courage it sometimes takes to focus deliberately and honestly on the sources of anger is a prerequisite to reconciliation as well as to meaningful protest, rightful resistance, and reform.

The "talking points" provided to participants in public arguments or protests are lists of reasons, strategies, reminders, demands, or objectives that help maintain clarity and consensus. Some, like those in the Declaration of Independence, offer lasting examples of righteous indignation. And we need these examples because we ought to be angry on behalf of those who have been systematically excluded, collectively blamed or shamed, killed because they lived in combat zones, or exploited in the service of others' wealth. We ought to be angry when we see ecosystems being destroyed or children demoralized or elders neglected or abused. There's plenty to be outraged about. And outrage generates energy, dangerous and potent like a surge of electricity, that can either fuel right action or lay waste what lies in its path.

Right action needs to be rooted in prayer, meditation, mindfulness—a willingness to step back and see the wider context of others' actions, and witness one's own performance in the drama from whatever distance allows a measure of equanimity, clarity, and unbiased judgment. It's hard to get there. Probably impossible without practices that keep avenues of grace and lines of communication open.

Surprisingly often, what begins as personal "spewing" may, in the process of finding adequate language for anger, become a process of clarification and discernment. If I begin with the simple fact that "this policy makes me furious," then give myself a chance to consider why, what particulars are most problematic, what specific effects it's likely to have, and what feasible alternatives might look like, I've successfully focused my spewing. And then if I make lists of both the objections and the alternatives, I become a more effective participant in public process.

At the protests and rallies I've attended, I've been both encouraged and amused to see the intelligence, wit, and resolve reflected on many of the signs people carry ("It's not about right vs. left, it's about right vs. wrong," "There is no Planet B," "Separate Church and Hate," "The Beginning is Near"). On those occasions I've also been impressed by how many have done the serious homework required to speak publicly not only with conviction, but with well-documented facts, statistics, arguments, and prophetic incisiveness about the implications of the policies or wars they're protesting. I've learned some valuable lessons from some of them about what to do with my own anger and frustration.

One thing to do, of course, is give it words. Words are one form of action, and we can't, in human communities, act for long without them. They are often the walls that protect precious places of silence. In the intimate sphere of family life as well as in the arenas of public debate or in board meetings or PTA meetings or church gatherings, allowing a space for anger before it erupts not only may defuse it, but may allow it to energize and deepen our collective will to live together in peace. So if you're angry, try making a few lists to see if they become channels where fury may be carried into the wider waters of reflection.

LISTS THAT LOCATE THE ANGER:

Why I think this indignation is righteous
What I need to defuse the fury
Why they might be angry
What keeps us at odds
How small irritants grew into big outrage

LISTS FOR LIFE REVIEW

Autobiography can take you anywhere. Your life material is yours to explore, play with, rearrange, weave, edit, or make into a song or a play or a legacy for children. Ira Progoff, whose "journal workshops" taught a whole generation of people how to learn from their own life stories, began each session with a listing exercise he called "Steppingstones." These were lists of ten steps or stages or moments in the history of a particular relationship, or in the life of your body, or in your intellectual development, or ten turning points or decision points or "aha" moments. Those lists of ten gave each participant points of departure for further reflection. You could pick one. You could pick three to focus on for the weekend. Or you could embark on a memoir the size of *War and Peace*.

Life review is a valuable periodic practice. Progoff pointed out—and I have had occasion to test this—that if you listed your significant moments every year, something in your history would shift every year because, as I mentioned before, "the past keeps changing." Our relationship to our stories, our understanding of what moments mattered and why, keeps shifting as we learn new lessons and age offers altered perspectives. We keep foregrounding and backgrounding because what matters on the day we decide to take a backward glance will give shape to the story.

There may be, as French writer Georges Polti famously speculated, only thirty-six plots, but the variations on our finite storylines are apparently endless. How boy met girl or what became of two sons' rivalry or the prodigal child or the orphaned siblings or the poor little rich girl or the victim child or even the wicked stepmother—these remain inviting questions no matter how many versions of their stories have been told. And our own lives, prosaic as they may sometimes seem, turn out to be as full of color and light as prisms, because our cracked and broken stories are, in fact, "where the light gets in."

We tell versions of these stories to our children, or our spouses, or our students, or our walking companions, or our therapists, or our pastors, or our dinner guests. The versions vary, though most of us don't deliberately lie. We omit for the sake of propriety, or privacy. Some secrets need to be told; others don't. But perhaps the most important version of our life stories we tell are those we tell ourselves.

It's worth noticing how we narrate our stories to ourselves. We can construct our life stories as narratives about loss, or discovery, or achievement, or about being found or changed or guided. We can tell them as stories about grace—what God has done in and for us. We can tell them as stories about forgiving and going on. We can get stuck in stories organized by guilt or shame, or in victim narratives that keep us and others fixed in confining roles from which we need to be freed. But we may need to tell the dark tales in order to release them and find our way to more empowering, life-giving versions. We may need to travel the self-perpetuating loops of blame until we find ourselves sufficiently tired of them to try another tack.

One of the functions of our sacred texts is to help us recognize ourselves as characters in a much larger narrative than our own. Sacred stories—biblical parables, myths, lives of prophets and priests and kings and saints— sometimes shock us into moments of deep recognition: I, too, have been forgiven; I, too, am kept from a larger life by many possessions; I, too, have been summoned by an angel.

A life review that begins with a simple list is like an archaeological expedition: shards of remembrance bring back whole scenes we had buried in memory, and offer them to us in new terms. Small moments acquire symbolic significance, and the process of sifting and sorting allows us opportunities to take possession of our lives. In her autobiography, *The Measure of My Days,* written when she was eighty-five, Florida Scott-Maxwell declared, "You need only claim the events of your life to make yourself yours. When you truly possess all you have been and done . . . you are fierce with reality." Naming is the beginning of possession. So below are a few invitations to life review that might help you name and reclaim and reorganize and recognize a life that, though you live it, is still steeped in mystery.

LISTS FOR LIFE REVIEW:

Moments of insight
When "where" mattered
Gifts from guides
What I edit out
What I no longer need to do

CRACKING OPEN CLICHÉS

Most of us roll our eyes (or resist the impulse) when someone plugs a cliché into an awkward conversational moment. Most of us get a little tired of hearing that "all's fair in love and war" or that a child is "as good as gold" or that some new gizmo is "the best thing since sliced bread."

And it can be deeply painful to hear, after a beloved parent has died, that "She's in a better place," even if we believe it's true, since the observation often serves as too ready a substitute for silence, or for a more authentic acknowledgment of the emotional complexity of the moment. Not that kindness has to be clever. Simple truths aren't always clichés; sometimes they're consoling or refreshing. The difference between those and clichés that quash emotional truths lies in whether they close down those felt moments or open them up to empathy and to whatever silence or conversation might occur.

Still, clichés wouldn't be clichés if there weren't truth in them. Benjamin Franklin's *Poor Richard's Almanac*, from which we inherit so many common sayings, was actually rather original in 1739. Those best known include "Haste makes waste," "A friend in need is a friend indeed," and "No gains without pains." For all their many reiterations, these are valuable teachings. But their value lies in how they're used. To use common wisdom wisely, we have to bring it into the complexities of the lives we know and live and see how and where it applies.

Listing can help us retrieve something of the wit and utility an old and dusty saying might actually have to offer. It can be a little like taking down an old volume that's not nearly as easy or enticing as the Internet, but discovering, as we page through it, a desire to sit down and read, slowly and thoughtfully, a passage that, in its very antiquity, offers something that meets a current need. So, if I ask myself, "What, in fact, are the virtues of 'early to bed and early to rise'?" I might find myself reflecting on my own sleep patterns, what happens when I'm up before dawn, when I feel most rested, what happens when I don't get enough rest, how I spend the hours of my day, what I know about my own circadian rhythms, and so on.

Or if I pause over the tired, end-of-day resignation in someone's voice as he sighs, "Another day, another dollar," I might consider what keeps the spirit alive in the course of a repetitive or mind-numbing work life and foster a more compassionate imagination for those who work in factories or tiny, dingy offices.

It's especially worth unpacking the clichés we find ourselves resorting to now and then, not only to nudge ourselves toward more precise and thoughtful observations, but also to find out what purposes they may be serving.

114

Below are a few one might subject to the slow scrutiny of a good list-maker.

CLICHÉS TO RECONSIDER:

When I've been "asleep at the wheel"
What might be needing "a stitch in time"
What it's going to take to get "back in the saddle"
When I "beat around the bush"
Where I might need to "blow the whistle"

WANTING WHAT YOU WANT

Years ago, as my daughter and I traveled across the country together, we listened to an assertiveness training course on an audio book. The teacher began by disabusing students of the idea that assertiveness meant being able to say No. Rather, she said, healthy assertiveness, the kind that fosters candor and trust, was essentially a matter of being able to identify and say what you want and, when necessary, take no for an answer. Her point was that if you know what you want and aren't afraid to ask for it because you're not afraid of the rejection that comes with a No, you can often have what you want. It reminded me of the biblical message, reiterated several times in Scripture, "You have not because you ask not."

That alone is an important teaching: simply, trustingly, to ask for what we want, as children would, is to be open to learning from what comes when we ask. It may be what we didn't know enough to want. It may direct our desires in a way that moves us toward greater spiritual awareness. But the teacher pointed out another problem people commonly encounter in asking for what they want, which is identifying what they want in the first place. What they *really* want, the desires of their heart. This kind of awareness takes time and attention. One good exercise is to ask ourselves, when a want comes up, "What's that really about?" What does that thing or experience or satisfaction represent?

Identifying wants, even the ones that seem frivolous or superficial (I want that bracelet, that pair of strappy shoes, the dessert that guy's having), is important not only because it may enable us to move closer to what really satisfies us, but because what we want gives us and those who love us valuable information. One exercise the teacher suggested was to go on a window-shopping trip with a beloved or a friend, taking no money or credit cards, for the sole purpose of pointing out what you want. And not, she made clear, so that your partner would then feel he or she needed to get you what you want, but so that you would know each other better. If I know what you want, I have a clearer sense of your attractions, affinities, tastes, hopes, and deeper longings. Small wants are often big ones in disguise.

Many of us are inhibited by messages we received early and often about not wanting too much, or wanting the wrong things. If our parents couldn't afford much, we learned not to ask. If speaking our wants was read as dissatisfaction, we may have been admonished and told to be grateful for what we had. But wanting isn't always the same as discontent: sometimes it's simply a movement of the heart or the unconscious that directs us toward our place of growth.

Of course, we live in a culture that besieges us with seductive messages inducing us to want things we don't need. Precisely because of that, it can be helpful to clarify the wants that come from within, recognizing that the real "desires of our hearts" can guide us in directions we need to go. And allowing ourselves to want what we want is an exercise of childlike freedom. Knowing we don't have to have exactly what we name, and that a want may be something to grow out of, we can be free to name all things, great and small, that appeal to us, from those that are simply flashy and glittery to those that are subtle and have lain unsuspected, but, when they surface, surprise us into new understanding.

Try a few of the lists below to discover what wanting has to teach.

WANT LISTS:

Things I wanted and never got
Things I want that I believe would truly enhance my
life and growth
Things I wish I didn't want
What I've learned about my wants
Things I used to want but don't anymore

TALKING POINTS

Whenever you decide to go public with opinions or proposals (and I recommend this—we need each other's voices and op-ed pieces), you need a list of talking points: things to be sure to mention, if you're asked. You also need these if the occasion calls for a brief, succinct, specific review of a controversial policy or decision. Or if your opponent is challenging your position and you don't have much time to cut her argument to ribbons. Good talking points usually include a few persuasive statistics or references to recent studies or precedents or pertinent news stories.

The practice of listing talking points isn't confined to debate teams or PR professionals. My daughter somehow took it up around the age of four. She would come into the kitchen after a stretch of unusual quiet in the other room and announce, "Mommy, I have three things to tell you." Then she'd lift three little fingers to emphasize her purpose. Sometimes the three things would be what she noticed that day about her baby sister or what happened at the Montessori school—generally including a report on a classmate of particular interest who, on a dare, would put a caterpillar on her tongue or eat glue. Sometimes the three things would be reasons why she should get what she had determined she needed—more time with a shared toy, the next volume in the *Little House* series, permission to make the frosting on the cupcakes blue. The habit served her well on the high-school debate team, and later when she learned negotiation in business school and subsequently practiced it with tough-minded teamsters.

Talking points can, of course, be used as shields or swords, and, when put to adversarial use, make open-hearted listening hard. But they can also enhance listening by fostering clarity and real understanding. Specifics are a measure of responsibility and care for truth. Vagueness is often a mark of ignorance, evasiveness, or inexperience—and it can be dangerous. We live in a historical moment when all of us need to be more attentive to how the Spirit is moving among us to reshape culture and revive a deeper common sense of things. I think of the admonition in 1 Peter 3:15 to be always ready to account for the hope that is in you. That seems to me to include being ready as well to account for our political affiliations, our choices of organizations to support, our volunteer commitments, and our decisions about how to spend time, energy, attention, and money.

Since there are places I won't shop or eat because I object to their treatment of labor or animals or the earth, it's good for me to be able to say why. Since I care immensely about education, I need to care about how it's funded and who's responsible for getting money to the right places, and I need to be able to talk with them if the opportunity presents itself.

However those opportunities arise, it's wise to be ready with talking points that might dispel confusions or misunderstandings, update old information, squash oversimplifications and stereotypes, and surprise a few people (including myself) into rethinking the issues.

TALKING POINTS:

What I've decided about my diet
What everyone needs to know about climate change

Why I won't allow you to stare at a screen for more than
two hours a day
Why I avoid shopping at _____
Why faith matters

THIN PLACES AND SACRED SPACES

Most spiritual traditions encourage some form of pilgrim-age—travel to a holy site, or a climb up sacred stairs to a shrine, or a walk into a clearing in the wilderness where God's presence becomes palpable. Moses went up the mountain to meet God. Jesus went out to the desert to pray. Irish Catholics climb Croagh Patrick. Hindus visit the Ganges. Sikhs go to the Golden Temple. Muslims travel to Mecca. The French host millions of pilgrims at Lourdes and the Mexicans at Guadalupe. And those who are not too faint of heart climb Machu Picchu.

Many pilgrims, religious or not, honoring the need to remember the dead and probe the mystery of our connec-tion with them, visit Hiroshima or the Vietnam memorial or the beaches of Normandy. And some, like T. S. Eliot, travel to sites on their journeys through family history that connects them with a past that is mysteriously present. One such journey took Eliot to a seventeenth-century Anglican chapel at Little Gidding, where he memorably reflected,

> You are not here to verify,
> Instruct yourself, or inform curiosity
> Or carry report. You are here to kneel
> Where prayer has been valid.

These beautiful lines remind readers that the purposes of pilgrimage may be, as Eliot put it, "beyond the end you figured, and . . . altered in fulfillment." We may not always know why we find ourselves persistently wanting to visit Iona or our grandfather's farm or St. Petersburg or the local cemetery, but I've come to believe that we should give such desires due regard.

The idea of "thin places" has been recently re-popularized by students of Celtic traditions, though clearly such places are universally recognized. The term comes from pre-Christian culture in Europe, especially Ireland, and refers to places where the separation between the world of the five senses and the subtle world just beyond seems to dissolve, and the divine seems more accessible. A strong sense of the presence of God, a heart-opening sense that one is being invited and addressed, a sense that the past is present and the cloud of witnesses gathered—all these mark a thin place. Some are personal; some are very public. No doubt any place can be a thin place when mind and spirit are open to such encounter, since God is the one "whose center is everywhere and whose periphery is nowhere." But it seems that in some places the energies of earth and heaven gather to open a special portal for divine encounter.

In one's own back yard, one might also discover a meeting place at the foot of a special tree. The practice of going to a particular place to pray, setting up an altar in a particular room, meditating on the bank of a favorite stream or by a window that opens onto a garden—these are common ways of finding, or establishing, a sacred spot in which to "practice the presence of God." To go there is an act of preparation, and of opening the mind and heart to deeper awareness, leaving distractions and preoccupations behind whatever threshold you cross to get there.

If you're stuck in a hospital room or confined to bed or in a workplace with little privacy, even this kind of "sacred space" may be hard to find. So the "place" you go may be in the mind, behind closed eyes and any closed door, for whatever minutes are available. Taking slow, deep breaths, repeating a centering word, holding a sacred object, or simply opening your hands to receive what is given can be enough to "make one little room an everywhere."

A list of "thin places and sacred spaces" can help open the mind and the spirit to this kind of experience. You can simply identify where you would go on pilgrimage if you could, where you have had moments of mystical experience or divine encounter or heightened awareness of subtle energies, where "prayer has been valid." See where one of these takes you:

LISTS OF SACRED SPACES:

Pilgrimage places I'd like to visit
Special rooms and sacred objects
Ancestral sites
Buildings that open my heart when I enter them
Natural objects I keep, hold, or visit

LOVE LETTERS

"How do I love thee? Let me count the ways" Elizabeth Barrett Browning famously asked, and then produced a sonnet full of answers—a list of "ways" any lover might rejoice to hear. Most of us could look at a beloved face, ask the same question, and come up with lists of our own, perhaps not in rhymed iambic pentameter, but in ways that might surprise and delight someone who doesn't expect such tribute.

It's not unusual for people nearing the end of their lives to offer this simple advice: If you love someone, don't neglect chances to say so. People need to hear it. It's not new information, but something more like a hug, a refreshing sip of water, a new bud on an old rosebush. And really, a simple "I love you" goes a long way. But for those of us who like to play with words, love letters can be an enjoyable challenge. Like graduation speeches or congratulations to new parents or other occasions that elicit clichés, love letters can be hard to craft out of the marshmallow-y substances to which they've been reduced in greeting cards and Valentine's Day ads.

Specificity is the key to a good love letter, and finding specifics is where the challenge gets interesting and fun. Fun is one good reason to write a love letter; it gives you as well as your beloved a lifted spirit. And we're not just talking here about a love letter to a spouse, but to a grandchild, an old friend, a former teacher we remember fondly, or even to God, where it flows into channels of praise.

In a digressive moment (of which I have many), thinking about this particular kind of list, I looked online and discovered a startling variety of sites dedicated to love letters. "Lovingyou.com" has an archive of love letters as well as a handy list of ways to write one. "Romancefor everyone.com" includes love stories as well, and a trove of ideas for readers seeking direction in writing about or to the beloved. "Loveletters.boston.com" dispatches daily advice to similar effect. A lot of us, apparently, want to find ways to "count the ways." These sites are no doubt helpful—even inspiring—but I also think a do-it-yourself approach to love-writing is likeliest to keep you close to the still small voice within you where a truth lies that only you can tell.

So, though I trust you could make up your own, here are a few prompts from me to you for love-lists to make to-day—because whatever day this is, it's a good day to write a love letter, beginning with some carefully chosen specifics:

LOVE LISTS:

Things I've thought but haven't said
What I noticed last time we went out
What I've missed since you've been gone
What I probably remember that you probably don't
What I see unfolding in you

LITANIES

I came to litanies later than friends who grew up with missals or prayer books. I was in college before I'd even heard of them. But I've come to love them. Though less commonly used in public than they once were, litanies are still recited on solemn occasions. Whether used specifically for prayer or simply as a recounting of concerns or of reasons to rejoice, the litany form allows us to slow down, dwell on, and dwell in what is on our hearts. The alternating rhythm of naming and refrain ("For rain in a dry season . . . we give thanks; for respite from pain . . . we give thanks") focuses awareness and soothes the spirit.

The term *litany*, of course, has come into wider, sometimes dubious use: we hear about people who appear regularly with a "litany of complaints," for instance. A supervisor might bring a litany of tasks to the morning meeting. A professor might recite a litany of titles one should have read before signing up for the class. In these contexts the word means little more than *list*, but it does retain a sense of ritual or ceremony that makes an occasion of the recitation.

The long lists of thanksgivings or petitions or blessings in formal litanies, crafted over time by generations of the faithful, offer a place of repose where words invite us to dwell in divine presence without "going anywhere" but here. They lead us into a space made of words that protects us for a time from the buffetings and distractions of the world. Among the "litanies approved for public recitation" by the Catholic Church are the "Litany of the Saints," the "Litany of the Sacred Heart of Jesus," and the "Litany of the Blessed Virgin Mary." Each of these offers a way for Catholics to enter into, explore, and deepen the heavenly fellowship they seek among the great "cloud of witnesses" who dwell just beyond the veil.

The Anglican "Great Litany" goes on at greater length than some might be inclined to enjoy, but I have come to think of it as an invitation and a challenge to "stay with" or "abide." It takes those who pray it on a rhythmic way through adoration, confession, petition, and final acts of complete trust, meditatively, without haste. It opens up caverns of awareness and long vistas on Christian history.

But my appreciation for traditional litanies doesn't prevent me from wanting to write my own. Writing litanies can keep our prayers or intentions current and sharpen our focus on particulars that need our deep attention. It's good to give a litany at least a couple of pages—enough space to stretch it beyond where it might begin to wane. Enough space to let new memories, feelings, and words surface. Enough space to let it change direction a few times. Consider, for instance, these variations on thanksgiving:

> For guidance in the surprises of each day, I give you thanks.

For health in a world where diseases abound, I give you
thanks.
For those you've given me to love, I give you thanks.
For the annoying people who are my teachers, I give you
thanks. . . .

Or these variations on situations:

In the frustrations of the workplace, may I learn
patience.
In the challenges of parenting, may I learn wisdom.
In the delights of friendship, may I learn generosity.
In the opportunities the day brings, may I learn
discernment.

Any list or litany can be developed by selecting a line
at a time and letting it be a starting point for further reflection. What do I mean by "wisdom"? Where have I witnessed or experienced wisdom? Or how has each of the
ways I've learned to name God opened up a new dimension of prayer? God has all the time in the world—time
for long lists, and for the silences between the lines, and
for our "struggle with words and meanings" that leaves
us always at the edge of the unspeakable—a shore where
we are invited to rest and simply enjoy the "beauty of
holiness."

By way of beginning, try adding some lines or making

some changes to this homemade litany and see where it
takes you:

> Knowing we are blessed
> in the beauties of ocean and hills,
> in the endless surprises of human kindness,
> in the peace that comes in spite of sorrow,
> > we bless you in turn, Creator God.
>
> For our greed
> that leads us to waste what we've been given,
> that leads us to kill time instead of redeeming it,
> that turns prudence to stinginess,
> > we ask forgiveness.
>
> For the gifts of this day,
> for the pauses between tasks,
> for music in the midst of traffic,
> for friends who are faithful,
> > we give thanks.
>
> For patience
> as we wait for healing,
> as a child finds her own way,
> as others take the time they need,
> > we ask you, who abides with us.

SUMMARY STATEMENTS

Summary is harder than it seems. Ask anyone to summarize the plot of a movie or a novel or the conversation at a committee meeting (that last being hardest because they may have been doodling on a notepad). What follows is often an unedited blow-by-blow or something so vague and generic that it leaves you unable to determine whether it's worth the cost of a ticket or the price of the book.

Summary requires a sense of the whole and discernment about what particulars matter most. It is selective and, when well-done, strategic. It is an effort to bring people up to speed or enable them to participate even if they come late to the conversation. Or an effort to clarify what's getting muddied in the swirling waters of commentary and speculation. Those who can summarize recent scientific findings about climate change or the content of a 3,000-page health-care bill or the state of the union perform important, time-sensitive, politically necessary acts of public service.

And most summaries, I would guess, begin with lists. They might simply be efforts to say "what happened." As any lawyer or doctor can tell you, questions like "What happened?" are deceptively simple. Do you want the answer in molecules? In family history? In a story about how you happened to be on the edge of the roof near the drainpipe when you fell? And then there are questions like "When did it start?" These seem to ask for a point in time: at least a dozen alternative answers might be offered. (You don't want to be my doctor—it's too time-consuming.)

For the very reason that they are so variable and rife with possibility, summaries are a salutary challenge. A simple practice to take on for a while (perhaps as a Lenten discipline?) might be to provide more engaging, thought-provoking, entertaining answers to "How was your day?" or "How's your mother doing?" or "How's it going?" All the ritual questions that we've reduced to little more than social gestures might be revitalized by short lists that summarize with a bit of style.

One of my dearest friends has a particular gift in this area. Anything the day offers can become a story. She can go to a soulless supermarket, buy the usual groceries, and come home with a story that makes the ordinary excursion into a small adventure. She doesn't invent; she just has a habit of seeing each particular encounter or event as an invitation to notice and reflect, and she accepts the invitations. If a homeless man asks her for money, if the cashier overlooked an item, if the car next to her was parked crookedly, if a child was whining for Cocoa Puffs, she has something to say about it. She seems to collect experiences as plot possibilities (as it happens, she's written twenty young adult novels), and she can summarize them so richly that I look forward to asking her, "How was your day?" Her conversation is a gift. She is ready to give a full and fascinating account.

Since it's an art so worth practicing, try it yourself. See what lists might emerge under the lines given below.

SUMMARY LISTS:

How the conflict developed
What's changed since I came of age
What my co-workers are hoping for
What I believe now
The eulogy I'd like someone to deliver

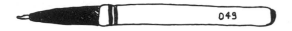

Part III

PLAY LISTS

All of us rely on other people's lists. In fact, some of them are foundational. Every tradition hands down some version of a list: the Ten Commandments, the eight Beatitudes, the four noble truths and the five great precepts of Buddhism, the five great Hindu precepts, the five pillars of Islam, the seven deadly sins, the seven spiritual works of mercy, the twelve steps and Twelve Traditions of Recovery. On a less exalted plane, our reliance on others' lists is evident in the regularity with which magazines feature lists as inducements to buy and read: Seven Ways to Destress; Ten Ways to Shrink Your Energy Bills; Twelve Ways to Make Money; Five Natural Ways to Help Your Health; Three Ways to Improve Work Performance . . . and so on. (These are all real titles.) We're all familiar with—and many of us are persistently attracted to—certain generic kinds of lists: how I found . . . (peace, happiness, the right partner); why I changed (my job, my mind, my exercise routine); what works (when you're dieting; when you're talking with teens; when you're redecorating on a small budget).

I don't think I'm alone in my curiosities about other people's lists. That curiosity is fed by a certain faith that where there are lists, a bit of wisdom or insight or good advice is likely to be found. Other people's lists surprise me and send me back to my own list-making with new inspiration to keep writing things down, let my own lists take new directions, and see what emerges.

In the spirit of sharing lists, I'm offering here a few of my own, and some short reflections on their birth and growth. I hope they'll provide a little amusement, a few templates or ideas to tinker with as you continue to think about how to make lists fun, timely, or instructive, or open up new windows onto your personal landscape. I invite you to try whatever they inspire you to try—imitation, variation, argument, invention. And I invite you to keep playing as you go. The open page where a list begins is wonderful play space—one of the many "fields of the Lord" that are ours to explore.

A LIST-MAKER'S MASTER LIST

Things to do no matter what
Things to do if I have time
Things to do badly if at all
Things to do when I've done everything else
Things to get someone else to do
Things to think about
Things to worry about
Things to fantasize about
Things to complain about
Things to be grateful for
Things to gloat about
Things to puzzle over
Things to plan
Things to postpone
Things to regret
Things to change
Things to learn
Things to leave alone
Things to buy
Things to buy only if they're on sale
Things to buy if I find them at a garage sale
Things to get rid of to make room for things to buy
Things to repair
Things to have someone else repair
Things to tolerate in disrepair

Books to read
Books I'll never read
Books to buy and maybe read
Books to have handy in case I break a leg
Books the children ought to read
Letters I want to write
Letters I ought to write
Letters I don't need to write if I call
People to forget
People to forgo
People to attend to
People to avoid
People to forgive

Perhaps this should serve as a warning to those who incline toward list-making: one day you'll find yourself making a list of lists to make. When that happens, it will be a sign that list-making has become a way of life, and a habit you won't easily relinquish. You'll have to make room for it. You'll have to buy notebooks or name new folders on your desktop. You'll begin to enumerate alternatives when given a choice, or to generate lists of things you barely paid attention to before, or to imagine lists other people should make. The only advice I can give to those for whom lists have taken on a certain compulsive quality is to have fun with them. Give up the *New York Times* crossword if need be, or Sudoku, and make lists instead. Scribble lists while waiting in line or waiting, phone in one hand, while AT&T finds someone to answer your call, which is very important to them.

As I began my "master list" of lists, I realized how powerfully parallel terms propel thought in a particular direction. "Things to . . ." or "People to . . ." or "Books to . . ." or "Letters to . . ."—and so on. Every category starts a cascade of possibilities. And as each item occurs, it suggests another. As I've said before, this is what's life-giving about list-making: there's always more. And more. And the more you add, the more you see that could be added.

Of course, "more" is not an end in itself, nor, for that matter, is a list. A list—even a copious and comprehensive one—is a beginning. Somewhere on it an item will call itself to your attention, invite further consideration, nudge you toward action, make you wonder, dare you to dare. On every list I've made, two or three lines have become trailhcads; they've led to conversations that needed to happen, or essays or poems or drawings, or, sometimes, dreams.

My list of lists is quite incomplete—a mere beginning. I include it here, and the lists that follow, as an invitation and encouragement to make your own.

Why read?

To rearrange what you thought you knew
To converse with unavailable people
It's cheaper than shopping
To restock your conversational larder
To counteract creeping media mindlessness
To see how others do it
To taste the flavor of words
For the joy of a graceful sentence
To get better-quality gossip
To discover new questions
To go places you can't get to otherwise
And come back changed

"Why" lists are a genre unto themselves. Once you ask "Why?" you begin to notice layers of need, motive, and cause that become more various and interesting the longer you stay with the question. One of the many features I have come to appreciate in William Faulkner's long, slow stories is how often he drops the reader into the middle of things with a sentence that starts, apparently randomly, with "Because. . . ." As though all our observations are part of an ongoing conversation in which "Why" sounds like a drumbeat underneath all urgencies and choices and is the taproot of story.

One can raise the why question anytime: Why go? Why

stay? Why bother? Why me? Why now? Why not? It generally offers as many answers as you can find the patience to
entertain. "Why?" can be an especially interesting question to raise about what might seem obvious. The answer
to "Why read?" seems so obvious that it could go without saying. The trouble with what "goes without saying,"
though, is that it doesn't. If one bothers to poke a little at
the obvious, then subtler undercurrents begin to stir, and
to disturb the smooth surface of the obvious.

So, why read? A serious and sensible—obvious—answer is that in a culture where every sort of empowerment
depends on basic literacy, illiteracy is a crippling disad-
vantage. That might seem a sufficient answer, but to stay
with the question is to let it lead you into rich reflection on
what happens when you read, and beyond the dangers of
illiteracy into the many specific rewards of literacy.

This particular list is a kind of autobiographical exercise, a reflection on my own reading life that began in a
family where reading was assumed and encouraged, and
that continued through an education and a career in classrooms where how to read and why were always the primary
questions. One of the effects of reading I still find most
valuable to emphasize is that it not only adds to what I
know, but "rearranges" it. When I read thoughtful writers—Wendell Berry, for instance, or Thoreau or Melville
or Toni Morrison, or Tolkien or Shakespeare or Lao-tse
or St. John—I am consistently surprised into reframing

some assumption or adjusting my angle of vision or re-examining an attitude.

Sometimes a single striking sentence will do it. One simple statement by George Steiner, author of *Language and Silence,* has informed my approach to language for decades: "Language is the defining mystery of man." I can't really take that in and fall back into thinking of words in simple utilitarian terms. And this sentence by Canadian writer Susie O'Brien permanently reframed my approach to environmental problems: "It's impossible to talk about the environment in a meaningful way without addressing the history of colonialism."

Sometimes even a word or a phrase encountered in a poem or paragraph accomplishes radical rearrangement. Recently I've been pondering a phrase I encountered in a *New York Times* review praising a writer's "generous lyricism," which brought back to mind another writer's term, "generous orthodoxy." Both add an affective dimension to what might otherwise be simply academic or theoretical ideas.

I can't talk to most of the writers I've learned from, but they are in very real ways my community. They, along with the folks with whom I share meals and phone calls, help grow me up and see me through. When I read, I enter into conversation; good reading isn't just a one-way street, as I learned early from inveterate writers of marginalia. I "talk back," I reread, and the text offers up new answers. Then, too, reading spills over into dinnertime conversations with real people in real time, moving us all beyond daily drivel, though there's a place for that.

Perhaps the best thing reading does is raise new questions, or old ones in new contexts. Why care? How do we know? What shapes our ends? The questions we ask change us. Thoreau's *Walden* changed me when I was sixteen, and again when I was thirty-five and teaching a course on American Romanticism, where I invited others to pause over the questions it taught me: What is necessary? Do we own our possessions, or do they own us? What might it mean to "stay awake" when "most men are asleep"? Why might so many be leading lives of "quiet desperation"? Toni Morrison's *Beloved* also changed me, helping me imagine the permeability of the veil that separates the living and the dead, the visible from the invisible, hope from despair. New translations of the Bible leave me changed: translators' word choices lead me to wonder about the difference between "kill" and "murder" or "charity" and "love."

Surprising, life-giving questions, more than answers, are the firstfruits of reading, and as my list of reasons to read led me back to them, I thought of Augustine's assertion that "The end of all things is delight." Or, as another writer put it, "radical amazement." That's my final answer to "Why read?": because occasionally, it gets you there.

AN INVITATION TO MY FELLOW LIST-MAKERS:

Here are several prompts for lists about reading:

Phrases that have stayed with me
Why read [your favorite author]?
Books I would retitle
The most enjoyable scenes in my reading life
My favorite nonfiction

What tennis teaches

Return to center.
Swing the racquet with your whole body.
Meet the ball in front of you.
Forgive yourself for a bad shot and get ready
    for the next one.
Don't watch your opponent—watch the ball.
Don't analyze while you play.
Hit the ball and let go of the result.
Bend your knees and stay flexible.
Accuracy matters more than power.
Skill matters more than equipment.
Toss the ball higher than where you'll be hitting it.

If you're playing the net, don't look back.
Stoop to meet the low ones.
Be consistent—and ready to change.
Don't let points interfere with play.
Revel in the moment of completion.
Play is not performance.

Sometimes lists about one thing tell you about something else. I've noticed that the lengthy conversations sports fans have—about players and plays, coaches and refs who made bad calls, how to position a ball for a free throw or put the strongest spin on a serve or catch a wave at the right moment—touch lightly but reliably on deeper concerns or values or hopes than are readily expressed. Sports, from the Super Bowl to the pick-up game in a sand lot, are simulations of life; each one offers its teachings about patience and precision and collaboration and loss and competition and play.

I wasn't raised in a sports-loving family. No one turned on Monday-night football in our household, or watched the Lakers games, or enjoyed the polite British courtside applause at Wimbledon. Until I discovered tennis in high school.

That discovery was revelatory. Tennis taught me all the things on this list, some of which I'm still learning, though I was never a star player, and a shoulder injury made me hang up my racquet some time ago. Tennis, it turned out, was a way of wisdom; playing it, I began to understand how body, mind, and spirit inform one another, not separable but deeply interrelated dimensions of human being.

What tennis taught me might also be learned, though perhaps with different emphases, from basketball or surfing or gymnastics or skiing. What the body learns, the mind turns into metaphor, or into parable, or into an organizing insight.

As I began to enumerate what tennis had taught me, I realized with renewed appreciation how valuable each of its lessons was. *Return to center*, for instance: After each shot, come back to the center of the court to get ready for the next. After every encounter, after every workday, satisfaction, or disappointment, return to center. Breathe. Meditate. Pray. Sit quietly for a few moments. Come home to yourself. Accept completion without belaboring successes, and setbacks without undue dismay.

Another good lesson: *Don't watch your opponent— watch the ball.* Comparison and competition lead to envy or crippling self-criticism. In "Sext," one of the deep, whimsical poems from Auden's *Hours*, the poet writes, "You need not see what someone is doing / to know if it is his vocation, // you have only to watch his eyes. . . ." He observes that those who are doing what they love have "the same rapt expression"—a beautiful "eye-on-the-object look."

Tennis legend Björn Borg had that look; half the pleasure of watching him play at Wimbledon was seeing the close-up of his eyes as he waited for John McEnroe's serve: focused, fierce, calm. To await any unknown—the next moment, the uncertain outcome, an answer, a revelation— in that way is to know that, though you never know what you're being prepared for, you can be prepared.

It was on the tennis court, too, that I learned a life lesson from my brother, whose occasional coaching had an added dimension of candor only a sibling could provide. As he watched my hardest serve go long yet again, he observed dryly, "Accuracy matters more than power." I don't know if he had any idea what a seed-crystal that sentence was. I have witnessed its truth in many an argument where invective and arm-waving deflate like a balloon in the face of factual evidence clearly presented. I think of its urgency when the airwaves get bloated with blather, and volume that passes for substance. It takes courage for scientists or historians or journalists or teachers or preachers or parents to step into the fray with simple, accurate, carefully validated, irrefutable information. When that happens, I think of the biblical story of David's five smooth stones. It took just one to fell Goliath.

But neither public conversation nor tennis is all contest. Play is the opposite of contest. Playful people don't clutch the scorecard. Play doesn't elevate outcomes over the delights of the moment—movement, grace, surprise, the deft angling, the subversive spin. Play, like love, doesn't show off, but takes deep pleasure in what is true and skill-ful for its own sake. Real playfulness is a return to a kind of innocence. And every sport can teach us something about becoming like a little child—open to the moment, open to what is life-giving in what is given, open to failing because forgiveness is always available, able to release this shot, this ball, this breath in trust, knowing the next will come.

AN INVITATION TO MY FELLOW LIST-MAKERS:

Pick a sport or craft or hobby or activity and consider what it has taught you, listing those things as they occur to you. Even the apparently trivial learning moments matter: learning to take small, even stitches in quilting; learning to bend from the waist in yoga; learning to offer or respond to slight pressure from your partner's hand when you dance. Assign yourself seven things, or ten, and then write a short reflection on how those learnings or lessons have served your deeper, more enduring purposes.

A manifesto for amateurs

It's worth doing badly.
It's about pleasure, not performance.
You don't have to keep score.
Delight is its own discipline.
Good work is play.
"Good enough" is sometimes good enough.
If you can hold a hammer, you can make a table.
It's okay to eyeball it.
Experts have their place.
But it isn't as big as we think.
Slightly crooked can be charming.
Slightly burnt can be tasty.
Love is attentive to what counts.
What counts isn't on the spreadsheet.
Don't let money undermine ecstasy.
The product is a byproduct.
Love the process.

As I get older and realize I'll never weave more than place-mats or play the flute in public, I take increasing pleasure in G. K. Chesterton's good-humored observation that "If a thing is worth doing, it's worth doing badly." One can experience surprising relief from the burden of youthful delusions once one gives up any notion of performing in Carnegie Hall or playing at Wimbledon or (perish the thought) becoming president. The message that "you can be anything you set your mind to," intended to inspire ambition in the young, can be quite oppressive. It's also not true. We all come into this world with certain gifts and limitations, the former to be developed as life allows, the latter to be overcome, perhaps, or perhaps accepted. Either way, they shape our ends with a certain inevitability, "rough-hew them how we will." We may become acknowledged authorities, celebrities, or experts in a field, but in the broader fields we wander through in daily life, most of us remain amateurs.

Amateur, from the Latin *amator,* is a happy word: it means "lover." What we aren't called to work at, we may be allowed simply to love. We can learn to play hymns or songs from our favorite musicals or "Bach for beginners" on the piano. We can make a quilt that won't be hung on anyone's wall, but may make a baby cozy. We can (with a little help) assemble a cabinet from IKEA even if we can't transform a tree into a dining table.

I began my "Amateurs" list in a certain spirit of celebration. Feeling encouraged—because I did in fact piece together simple squares for a very inexpert quilt for a very small, uncritical child—I wanted to write a list of encouragements for others of "a certain age" who might be coming to terms with their own dwindling ambitions and modest talents. Some of the items on the list are explicit permissions I have learned to grant myself and others. "It's okay to eyeball it," for instance, applies to the amount of coffee I shake into the cone filter (more or less three scoops), or the amount of cinnamon I put in the pie (several good shakes, and then one more, because I like cinnamon), or the place on the wall where I drive the nail (about where it looks right) to hang another of my husband's playful paintings.

And "You don't have to keep score" represents a happy moment in my history of mediocre but enjoyable hours on tennis courts. With a certain elation, I realized I didn't have to aspire to tournament play, or even to winning matches, but could wander up to the courts with a like-minded friend and just hit the ball. I realized that what I loved about tennis was the feel of the ball meeting the "sweet spot" on the racquet, and the stretch of my body when I managed to meet the ball at just the right moment.

I learned that "the product is a byproduct" when I first read Maria Montessori's beautiful books about child development, where she speaks of the deep place of peace and wisdom one reaches by doing a thing for its own sake, allowing the process to be the reward. The product may be for someone else, or it may be a piece of refrigerator art with a very short half-life. But the process inscribes its patterns in the psyche and the cells. Montessori offered me permission to enter into my projects for the sheer love of the work, letting the goal go in the long meantime. That permission got me through graduate school; the degree that came at the end was often the furthest thing from my mind, but the hours I spent with Aeschylus and Thoreau and Melville and Morrison and even Milton felt like life deeply lived, in intimate—not secondhand—conversation with teachers I came to love.

An important feature of amateur endeavors is that they generally don't involve money. My husband often quotes his grandfather, who was fond of reminding him, "It's amazing how much you can get done if you don't care who gets the credit." In the same way, it's amazing how much we can do and enjoy and contribute and learn if we don't care about getting paid. Of course we have to make a living, and of course "the workman is worthy of his hire" (and the working woman!), but even for those of us striving to make ends meet, I believe there need to be corners of our lives in which we spread out our projects or set up our art tables without thought of profit. Those are small retreat spaces where we can "become like little children" and play for sheer pleasure.

Because of my long teaching career, there are areas in which I can speak with some authority about educa- tion or American literature or language. I'm grateful to have opportunities to do work I love and be paid for it. But when I wrote and occasionally now reread my "Mani- festo for amateurs," I find myself equally grateful to have lived long enough to enjoy short walks down roads not taken—to learn some things about medicine, take a class in Tai Chi, venture into vegan cooking, discover a few inspiring science writers, watch documentaries about things I never studied in school. Manifestos empower people. I encourage you to write your own.

AN INVITATION TO MY FELLOW LIST-MAKERS:

One general definition of a manifesto is "a public declaration of policy or aims." Try writing one, including intentions, insights, permissions, and a few challenges to "common sense." One of these, for instance:

A manifesto for moms (or dads or grandparents)
A manifesto for the Sunday-morning faithful
A manifesto for Monday mornings
A manifesto for the family cook
A manifesto for the electronically overwhelmed

See what happens when you combine serious intention with irony or amusement; varying the tone may serve more than stylistic purposes.

How to defeat bureaucracy

Know what you want.
And why.
If the right person isn't listening,
    talk to the wrong person.
Know your own terms.
Laugh.
Don't use their jargon.
Recognize bureaucrats as fellow victims of the system.
Ask their names and use them.
Do it their way when their way makes sense.
Repeat your point as often as needed.
Add marginal comments to their completed form.
Replace the information they requested
    with the information that matters.
Don't appeal to common sense: model it.

How-to lists appeal to most of us because most of us need and want specific guidance about how to parent, lose weight, manage our money, assess news outlets, contact our legislators, make a perfect pie crust, grow begonias, live more simply, or organize against abuses of power. Writing a how-to list isn't necessarily a claim to expertise; sometimes it's simply a way of clarifying for ourselves the steps we might need and want to take—ordering, winnowing, and considering priorities as we go.

Rather than paying slavish attention to how someone says we should write, it might be more helpful to notice how we do write. Writing our own how-to list is a way of assuming authority over our own processes.

Living, as we all do, somewhere on the complex grid where multiple bureaucracies intersect, I found it important one morning to spend a little time considering how not to capitulate entirely to the increasingly bureaucratic processes imposed upon us by the "powers that be."

Bureaucracies proliferate. They do so often to the point of defeating the original purposes their many offices were meant to serve. Most of us have spent precious hours of our lives listening to recorded messages that direct us to "press #1" to get to the next message, which will similarly direct us to press a number for more information—or for further delay. Most of us have also had frustrating conversations with middle managers who aren't authorized to address our complaints, but who unfortunately can't connect us with their supervisors. Or we end up struggling to communicate with "support staff" who, in the line of misconstrued duty, end up impeding rather than supporting what they were ostensibly hired to support. While not all administrative hierarchies harden into a maze of barriers, too many do.

So I thought about my most frustrating encounters with bureaucratic procedures, most of which involve copious and redundant forms to fill out, unnecessary yet required reports to be written for people unlikely to read them, and inane conversations with people at desks who serve as buffers between the people in charge and the rest of us.

I've discovered that one key to penetrating bureaucratic barriers is clarity: "Know what you want" is an instruction I learned to give myself before picking up the phone or walking into an office or even crafting an e-mail. Venting frustration may serve an immediate purpose, but it rarely brings about change. Clarity about my own purposes, values, plans, and priorities actually has, at times, enabled me to reshape the conversation with those in charge—a few times with surprising long-term effect.

Once, as a department chair, I objected to the utterly pointless redundancy of an end-of-the-year report that reported on what we had reported on during the year when we distilled minutes from meetings which, themselves, constituted adequate reports. So I called the administrator in charge of collecting the report about reports, told her why I thought it was pointless, told her what I thought I should be doing with my time instead, and said, as politely as I could, that I would not be submitting the report. I didn't blame her: please note that I include in my list the importance of recognizing, with some compassion, others caught in the same thicket, even when they contribute to the problem. But I was very clear about what I intended to do and why. I followed through and didn't submit the report. And here's the thing: Nothing happened. There were no repercussions. I can't promise that would always be the happy outcome of a carefully considered act of protest, but it did teach me a lesson about clarity that has served me well on subsequent occasions.

By means of similar experiments, I've also learned to talk to the "wrong person" if the "right person" is persistently unavailable. This might mean "going over someone's head"—an institutional impropriety that occasionally deserves to be dared. Or it might mean talking to someone competent to get a small job done without the disproportionate delay of a work order that has to be rubber-stamped by several intermediaries before reaching the guy with the toolbox. It might mean hatching a plan with one's disgruntled fellow workers or shoppers and organizing a bit of collective action rather than filling out the individual complaint form. At the very least, it means taking a few moments to consider the rationale for whatever procedures frustrate our purposes. If the purposes have merit, the procedures need to honor them.

And if they have merit, they deserve to be articulated at every point in the process. The "information that matters" often gets lost in the process of supplying information that doesn't. I learned this and other valuable lessons years ago from a small, readable book, *The Death of Common Sense* by Philip Howard, an attorney who has spent a good deal of time and print on bureaucratic and legalistic absurdities.

In law, in medicine, in education, in customer relations, in political debate, and certainly in social media, information that matters can easily be buried under information that satisfies abstract standards or obsolete requirements or someone's need to justify his or her job by generating more pages of print.

Especially in a climate where misinformation and disinformation proliferate, it matters to exchange information that matters in clear sentences, clearly delivered, when the moment calls for clarity. And clarity requires courage. And courage may be sustained by, among other things, a sense of humor. One way to defeat bureaucracy when it threatens to defeat what we care about is to laugh—not in mockery, necessarily, but in the freedom we maintain when we keep one foot outside institutional boundary-lines and, from that margin, keep a critical eye on how things work.

AN INVITATION TO MY FELLOW LIST-MAKERS:

Make a how-to list for yourself, considering as specifically as you can what's involved in a process that matters to you, even if you feel you're not sure exactly how to approach it. For example, you might consider how to take on problems like these:

How to manage electronic overload
How to disappoint people and still like yourself
How to get out the door on time
How to use insomnia to your advantage

Or you might simply see how well you can articulate a process others might find baffling:

How to get an item on the city council's agenda
How to get reliable news and avoid information overload
How to have an inner life when your outer life is
fully booked

What's fun after fifty

A new bud on the rosebush
Mozart with your feet up
Playing the same nocturne again, only better
Rereading Tolstoy
Not having to win the tennis match
Or arm wrestle
Avoiding amusement parks
Not being nineteen
Feeling entitled to irony

Enjoying one's eccentricities
Knowing how
And when
Doing it your way
Satisfactions the young don't even suspect

As more and more of my friends have turned fifty, the matter of how to live the "second half" of life (though that term presumes a very long life) becomes a more frequent topic of conversation. Aging baby-boomers provide a big market for articles and courses and advice about aging. We expect to do it longer, and hope to do it more healthily than our parents or grandparents, though we may, ironically, find ourselves stressing about how to "age successfully."

I recall an amusing conversation with our thirteen-year-old one day, in which I suggested that, actually, forty was more fun than fourteen. He was clearly skeptical. Obviously, I was trying to make the best of a sad situation. I was tempted to quote David Mamet: "Age and treachery will always overcome youth and exuberance." But I didn't. I did, however, write a poem, perhaps to confirm for myself, if not convince him, that my claim really corresponded to my own sense of the gifts of age. Among the lines I remember best from that exercise are these:

> He doesn't believe me, thinks the best
> it can get when you're old as that

is the consolation of power—
the privilege of telling someone else
to take out the trash.
"Fun" is a small word. He can have it.
I'll take contentment, serenity, satisfactions
sprinkled like raisins in daily bread. . . .

Later, though, I reclaimed "fun"—largely because it's been one of the great gifts of my ongoing adulthood to have known a fair number of elders who *are* having fun. One danced the Charleston to a live band at her eightieth birthday party. One wrote her third and fourth novels in her seventies. One takes adult-ed courses on an astonishing range of topics, reveling in learning she didn't have time for in her twenties. These friends have given me a great respect for fun—especially for the way that term becomes more capacious as it widens to include the deep, quiet, interior pleasures that often go unrecognized.

My list of what's fun after fifty came to me on a happy afternoon not long after my fiftieth birthday. Remembering the poem about the fun of being forty, I considered, as I puttered along in more than usual contentment at small Saturday tasks, what fun it was to do what I was doing. I did, in fact, spot a new bud on the rosebush that gave me a sudden rush of pleasure—somewhat undeserved, since I'm not, in fact, a meticulous keeper of roses. (My plants—the ones that survive—have lived lives of resilient

161

forgiveness.) Inside, my husband, also in his fifties, was playing a piece on the piano that I'd heard him practice many times. He played it slowly, deliberately, doing it, I imagine, for his own purposes, which had nothing to do with performance.

He and I had reached that season of companionship when not everything has to be commented upon, when habits are known, laughed over, tolerated, and cherished, when shared enjoyments had come to include a good many very simple things: big salads and backgammon at dinnertime; being read to while cooking or cleaning up; lingering over coffee in the early morning no matter how busy the day was likely to be.

As I added items to the list of things I've found to be fun after fifty, I came to see more clearly how many of them had to do with permission—not to do what wasn't really fun anymore; to take time for small satisfactions; to laugh, sometimes up our sleeves, over others' follies and our own; to take genuine pleasure in what we know now. Along the way, we have learned things. We know we don't have to invent the wheel or prepare for a Nobel acceptance speech. And that self-knowledge, it turns out, gives us a good deal of satisfaction. It means we can relax and have fun. I was an earnest child, raised with a strong work ethic and urged to achieve. So the wisdom of fun—permission to play, and to play my way—was a long time coming. I'm having it now. And one of the many fun things I do is make lists.

AN INVITATION TO MY FELLOW LIST-MAKERS:

Consider fun. Consider what's not fun. (As a friend of mine wryly observed on irritating occasions, "This is not fun. I've had fun. This is not it.") Consider what's become fun only recently. Or what you can't believe you're enjoying now because you would have hated it ten years ago. And see where one of these lists takes you:

> *Fun I never thought I'd have*
> *Slightly guilty pleasures*
> *Why it's fun to spend time alone*
> *"Fun" I don't have to pretend to have anymore*
> *Deepening pleasures*

What marriage teaches

There's more than one way.
What "goes without saying" doesn't.
There are no "isms" in intimacy.
Love requires imagination.
Laughter heals.
Taboos are toxic.
A hug provides more energy than a vitamin pill.

"Apologize" is an active verb.
Act I happened before you came on stage.
Freud was right.
And wrong.
Mothers matter.
Not everything can be shared.
What can be should be.
The subtext may be more important than the plot.
Mistakes turn out to be gifts if you open them up.
You learn what works by forgiving what doesn't.
If you're out of sync, you may be learning
    a new dance step.
Flowers don't fix things, but they help.
If you're not still being surprised, you've fallen asleep.
It won't be exactly what you bargained for.
Steady and exciting are not mutually exclusive.
The little things are the big things in disguise.
Love is bigger than understanding.

The only one of Shakespeare's sonnets that doesn't move me as it's supposed to is one of the most popular. The extravagant claim in Sonnet 116 that "Love is not love that alters when it alteration finds" and its insistence that "Love is an ever-fixed mark" seem far less true or useful than Wendell Berry's gentle, paradoxical observation, after years of faithful marriage, that "Love changes, and in change is true." Married love has to change, I have found, to make room for family, for each spouse's spiritual restlessness or creative growth or late-blooming ambitions, for injury and its aftermath, for losses, for the subtle coming of new seasons.

Several times I've had the privilege of joining my husband, who is a pastor, in pre-marital counseling conversations with young people who have asked, with touching humility and hope, for our guidance. We give it, knowing also how much we don't say in those tender moments about the bumps and turns and trials and fresh starts and unwelcome surprises that years of marriage can bring. We do recommend prayer and laughter and date nights and times of solitude and regular, leisurely, open-hearted conversation.

In the course of our own conversations about these conversations, I began writing down my own list of things that marriage teaches. It has taught me, sometimes more belatedly than I would have wished, and at some cost, things I'd like an elder to have told me earlier. That the little things are the big things in disguise, for instance: small irritants need to be attended to, or the wispy, persistent wishes that cloud the edges of consciousness. Or that what one may regard as a silly and dispensable holiday ritual, the other may look forward to all year. Or that building trust requires toughening up enough to confront one's partner.

Making a list of what marriage has taught and continues to teach me—longer than the list here, a record of lessons learned I keep for my own reflections—has helped me locate my own learning edge as the years of marriage lengthen and enter new seasons. The bits of advice on it come from the "inner wise woman." She's in there, though she hides in her cave a good bit of the time. She's the one who told me with a crooked smile that "It won't be exactly what you bargained for." It's good to listen for those wise ones who lurk and watch; they remember when we forget. It's also good to listen for the voice of the child in me who wants a present to unwrap now and then or an outing or a sudden hug for no apparent reason.

Keeping this list helps keep both the inner conversation and the conjugal conversation clear and pointed and personal. Nowhere is it more important to put names to feelings or hopes or close observations than behind the doors that define the bounds of domesticity and the spaces within which we work out our salvation, sometimes with fear and trembling, sometimes with a glass of wine or over scattered sections of the *New York Times*. It may be that some version of what marriage teaches should hang on the bedroom wall, perhaps with a pen nearby so new lines can be added from time to time. Because the learning, God willing, goes on.

AN INVITATION TO MY FELLOW LIST-MAKERS:

Adapt the list of things marriage teaches to reflect your own (perhaps on the occasion of an anniversary): "What this marriage has taught me."

Consider one of the life practices marriage has taught you and expand it. For instance, if marriage has taught you to hold your peace a little longer, you might try a list called "What I've learned to wait for"—again, as a gift to surprise a spouse.

Or feel free to write a campy, funny, satirical variation— maybe "What I've learned not to do." Though I make this suggestion with a reminder not to make the edges too sharp!

Other mothers

The woman who taught you to read
The babysitter who played with you
    instead of watching TV
The woman next door who came to your piano recitals
The boyfriend's mom who still liked you
    after you broke up
The old woman at church who prayed for you

The auntie who knew how it was when Mom didn't
The childless aunt who gave you her gift of mother-love
The teacher who tutored you on her own time
The librarian who remembered what kind of books
    you liked
The Girl Scout leader who listened to you giggle all night
The professor who midwifed your intellectual rebirth
The woman who clued you in when you were
    a newcomer at work
The woman who mentored you through
    your first pregnancy
The eighty-year-old elder who is your midlife role model
The stepmother who wasn't wicked after all

Writing life reviews like this can lead us into a deep glen of gratitude. Once the category of "mothering" begins to open up, a wide variety of contacts and relationships present themselves in that light. Similar lists might be made of father figures, people who showed up, teachers who stood at the turning points, or chance encounters—people we met once and never forgot.

As I began to write this list, I discovered that every line commemorated a particular woman who helped me on my journey. I also discovered that I'd been "mothered" throughout my life, and that "mother" is a verb. Let me hasten to say that, by the grace of God, I had a wonderful mother who rooted and grounded me in faith, fostered my intellectual curiosity, read me *Little Women*, told formative stories about working with orphans in India, and managed to laugh even when money was scarce and needy neighbors called at inconvenient hours.

I also had a delightful live-in grandmother who read me *Winnie-the-Pooh*, showed me how to peel apples, taught me to recite Psalms (King James Version only), and brought a bit of old Virginia into our small L.A. stucco house. So one might think I didn't need "other mothers." But I did—we all do.

From a historical perspective, the nuclear family is an oddity. For most of history, most people were handed around as children and learned early to recognize whole circles of elders as aunties and uncles whom they could trust in a pinch and consult when perplexed, and with whom they shared the ties that bind.

In recent years, a narrow "focus on the family" has been fostered by a wide bandwidth of well-meaning Americans, but when widened beyond the nuclear unit, family becomes spacious and rich with variety. We begin to consider and be grateful for those whom we have been given.

Themes emerge as we think about the people who have mattered. If you had a musical upbringing, the ones who taught you to sing or hold an instrument or listen closely to birdsong might come first in your hall of heroes. Or if sports have taught you the lessons that have served you on the court and off, coaches will show up on the list, and older siblings who took the time to shoot baskets with you, and the grandparent who bought you your first bat. In my family, reading was valued and practiced and talked about at the dinner table.

That's why my list started with "the woman who taught you to read," because it was the first thing that came to mind when I began to think about my "other mothers." The women who taught me to read merit a list of their own: Mom and Grandma; Mrs. Hinkson in second grade, Mrs. Matson in ninth; Dr. Jordan, who ushered me through *The Odyssey*; Mme. Crosby, who introduced me to Montaigne; and my beloved mentor, Jo, when I began my own career in college teaching. Learning to read, read more deeply, read more imaginatively, more critically, more receptively—this is an ongoing process, like learning to listen and discern.

And here's another thing about list-making that I learned from this list: items on a list often generate new lists. Let them. Sometimes making lists within lists, we find ourselves with a whole lovely series of nested lists that reveal and articulate long-buried layers of memory or awareness.

As the list of "other mothers" emerged, particular kindnesses came to light as forms of mothering, received from women whose attention extended well beyond what might have been required (the babysitter, the boyfriend's mom, the old woman at church, the watchful librarian). Suddenly a whole circle of women who hadn't known one another became for me a little communion of saints.

Inventories like this one tend to fall into chronological order, though they don't need to. Surveying my history with other mothers, I began to think of those who have served that role in my adult life when I still needed mothering. (Though it's a seldom-acknowledged fact, we all still do.) Some writers speak about "mothering oneself"; that phrase doesn't quite inspire confidence in me, but that there is a wise woman in my psyche who can help me when I need her has proven to be a valuable teaching. All the women on the list have helped bring that wise woman to life.

This is the woman who has helped me step into what I think of now as the "elder space" we get to enter and occupy if we live long enough. She has helped me be the mother I'm still being for my adult daughters. She's also helped me be an "other mother" for some of the lovely, lively younger folk who have been given to me to nurture, teach, mentor, and enjoy: students, sons and daughters of friends, aspiring writers, young teachers seeking tenure, and my stepchildren, who, after some consideration, seem to have decided that I wasn't wicked after all.

AN INVITATION TO MY FELLOW LIST-MAKERS:

List your "significant others"—mothers, fathers, teachers, guides, instructive adversaries—by name, including one thing they did for you that was formative in some way. Here are a few examples:

Auntie Ruth, who showed me that good humor can have
    an edge
Mrs. Robidart, who bought more Girl Scout cookies than
    she could eat
Louisa May Alcott, with whom I spent many happy
    hours in my treehouse
Mrs. Hinkson, who began every class with a song
Jo, who held up a mirror when I needed to see

Where the Spirit moves

Along hiking paths
And among high-rises
In the swell of waves
And in their breaking
In the oncology center
And the delivery room

Between book covers
Beside the wanderer
Among the mall rats
In suburban kitchens
And Afghan caves
In the conversations of committees
And the musings of monks
In every breath
Including the last

"Bidden or unbidden, God is present." This reassuring reminder has helped me through times when I have found my own prayer life, and consequently my felt sense of God's presence, eroding from fatigue or distraction or doubt. I dwell, in spite of my dithering self, in the presence of God. All I have to do, as Denise Levertov so beautifully put it, is fall "into Creator Spirit's deep embrace."

Over the years since my careful, caring upbringing by evangelical parents, I have found myself focusing at different times on different persons of the Trinity, and more recently on a wide range of ways to become aware of and enter into divine presence. Leaning into the mysterious words that I first encountered in King James' English, the Spirit "bloweth where it listeth," I think increasingly of God as hanging around, showing up, walking with, dwelling among, entering into, lurking, surprising, awaiting, accompanying. Four sentences came to me one day in prayer and have stayed with me like a refrain that sings me through even the darkest days: You are held. You are witnessed. You are accompanied. You are loved.

If these things are true for me, I believe they're true for each one of us. The Spirit "bloweth" into a lot of dark corners. Tattooed pastor Nadia Bolz-Weber, woman of wild words and emphatic faith, entitled one of her books *Accidental Saints: Finding God in All the Wrong People.* In it she reminds readers in salty specifics about who, exactly, Jesus chose, unconventionally, to eat with and talk with and heal. Those thought of as unsavory and un-deserving sorts. Like the above-mentioned "mall rats," for instance. Jesus and the Spirit can also be found in other dark places—deathbeds, rooms where severely de-pressed people have drawn the shades, boring gatherings of bureaucrats, and ancient rocks where children hide from gunfire.

It's a good exercise to name the people and places where God is likely to show up. The list becomes a kind of credo. Every added line drives home this truth about divine abundance: there's more. And then there's more.

Asking forgiveness for his many sins in a poem I can only call a joyful confession, John Donne concludes each confessional stanza with this refrain: "When thou hast done, thou has not done, for I have more." More sins to confess, more forgiveness to receive.

Every specific in the lists we write evokes a response. As

our lists grow—confessional or celebratory, exploratory or evocative, what we keep finding out is this: there is more. More grace, more fun, more possibilities, more facets, more reasons, more to let go of, more to learn.

AN INVITATION TO MY FELLOW LIST-MAKERS:

Consider specifically where the Spirit has moved in your life and through your days and adapt the above list to make it a personal inventory of awareness.

Rename the list and develop it in a slightly different direction—"Where grace has been given" or "When God showed up" or "Small surprises that made a big difference."

Imagine rewriting this list with a particular person or situation in mind—as a message of comfort for someone who is ill; as a bit of religious instruction for a child preparing for confirmation; as a celebratory retrospective for a significant birthday.

APPENDIX

A Few Final Lists for Your General Enjoyment

What the beach teaches

The next wave will come when this one goes.
There's a lot to be gained from building a castle
    that will crumble at the next high tide.
If you dive into the wave, it won't overwhelm you.
One man's sacred spot may be another man's
    volleyball court.
A lot will disappear by tomorrow.
Or be replaced.
Or rearranged.
Things take time.
They endure.
Bare feet quicken the senses.
What yields and what endures are not opposites.
Birds who compete when they feed
    cooperate when they fly.
What recurs is new each time.

Again and again is not tedious.
Sand teaches sculpting, detachment, and humility.
Erosion is an art form.
Found art should be left where it's found.
We're blessed, but not needed.

What weddings require

Redrawing the mattering map
Miss Manners
Resurrection of long-lost relatives
Embarrassing family stories
Compromise
Separation of church, state, and family members
Advice from an army of experts
And a friendly herd of amateurs
Finding a bridesmaid's dress that flatters every body type
Coming to terms with his questionable taste
Coming to terms with her whimsy
Discovering how tradition matters
Or doesn't
A long look at in-laws
Conversing with self-appointed stand-up comics
Deliberating over differences among fabrics

And flowers
Trying to protect what is private
Bad jokes
Time for tears
Seating charts and other peace-keeping strategies
Gratitude that survives 300 thank-you notes

The benefits of bicycling

Clean air
Thighs of iron
Sweat
Sailing through traffic jams
Sounds and smells
Cheap tune-ups
No line at the gas pump
The joy of long downhill slopes
The challenge of long uphill slopes
The good guys at the bike store
Little clip and zipper gadgets
Baby seats
Seeing more than the joggers
Hearing more than the motorcyclists
Coming home renewed

When to call home

When life is hard
When it isn't
When it's too early to call anyone else
When you have cosmic questions
Or want to know how long to cook pasta
When you need an over-forty point of view
When you wish to be celebrated
When you need a reality check
Or permission to dream
When no one else would get the punch line
Or put up with you in certain moods
Or just enjoy the sound of your voice
When you're homesick
And when you're not

Why children enchant us

They don't know their lines.
They don't consider the consequences.
They remind us of life before irony.

They invent logic.
We know more than they do.
We've forgotten things they know.
We know when they're pretending.
They can be surprised by the obvious.
They're very small.
They find laughter in odd places.
They think the commonplace is curious.
They aren't yet convinced that fun requires electricity.
They're not in it for the money.
They like the sound of words.
They don't mind singing in the street.
They're washable.
They get that grandma is beautiful.
If they're afraid, they'll tell you.
They think a question is a good way to find out.
They think it's okay to sleep wherever you get sleepy.
They don't kid themselves.

Where to dance

In the aisles
Down the halls
Before the altar

In your nightgown
On the balcony
In the kitchen while things simmer
In the street on July 4th
On the beach
In the empty classroom in June
In the office on weekends
On the playing fields after the game
In the nursery with small children
In the nursing home with your grandmother
At the airport before you say good-bye
At the rest stop off the highway
In a bar in Texas
At a ball in Vienna
On stage
And back stage
While you're waiting at the bank
In line at Safeway
"Upon the greeny grass"
In a canoe—carefully
Under the stars
Or the sun

What you get from a garden

Visible gratitude
Small surprises
Metaphors
A place to think
Antidotes for too much thought
A place to slash and burn and feel good about it
A dozen shades of green
Solvable problems
More than you put in
Permission to be muddy
A chance to see the whole cycle of seasons
A feast of color
Encounters with interesting creatures
Patience
Zucchini for the whole neighborhood

How to be happy in high school

Sit where the listening is good.
Find friends in odd places.
Get to know the good teachers.
Use the bad ones for character study.

Find a lunch table with a view.
Practice loving learning.
Try something new every week.
Test your limits.
Audition often.
Notice the people others overlook.
Assume there's a gift in every assignment.

What leaders learn

Leaders know their limits.
A good hand-off is as good as a touchdown.
The whole is bigger than the sum of the parts.
A good hunch may come from a questionable source.
Good ideas don't always come from where
   you expect them.
You can't lead without listening.
Claiming appropriate authority is as important as
   questioning authority.
Humility is not the same as abdication.
Appreciating others' gifts is as important as
   exercising your own.
The slowest, quietest, or most confused may be
   a key player.

Well-managed conflict may be as useful as
   well-kept peace.
Sometimes leading involves following.
Power is not the key term.
Don't pretend you don't have power.
Reframing releases creative energy.
Productivity isn't the only relevant unit
   of measurement.
You have to be willing to disappoint and displease.
You can't make allies without alienating someone.
Creative compromise works better than
   complete consistency.
Self-selection usually works.
Coercion usually doesn't.
What looks like laziness may be germination time.
Delegation is a discipline.
Take the heat.
Cover-ups are a bad idea; discretion isn't.
Balance predictability and surprise.
Be ready to rotate out at the right time.

Listen

To the hum of insects
To the cries of the poor
To the Spirit who speaks in silence
To your dreams
To your heart
For the lesson
To the voices of morning
For the word you need
To waves
To Bach
To the very young and the very old
To the beat of the dance
Through the noise to the music

A manifesto for moving day

If it's been in a box since the last move, you can let it go.
Puzzles without pieces are pointless.
The velveteen rabbit will not become real.
Bits of unidentifiable hardware are not
    potentially useful.
Now is the time to retire the single socks.

You don't have to clean it before you pack it.
Other people's stuff is easier to sort.
Even though your mother saved your Girl Scout hat,
    you don't have to.
What might be useful someday more likely won't.
Sentimental values are inflated.
Walden is worth rereading.
You don't have to keep the tasteless ties.
The moving guys are stronger than you are.
Sometimes it's better not to supervise.

What every adult should be able to do

Diaper a baby
Change a tire
Make soup with what's available
Sew on a button and hem a cuff
Converse with a stranger
Tell an entertaining story
Talk about faith
Write a letter of condolence
Sit with the sick
Say no to salespeople
And to cute children

Argue without fighting
Imagine why someone might like opera
Teach a child to read
Say why
And how
Be the place where the buck stops

What teachers can tell you

Attendance can be regulated; learning can't.
Teaching is art; learning is grace.
You can't always tell who's having an epiphany.
Allow for surprises and you'll get some.
The real results can't be quantified.
You can't learn when you're angry.
Or hungry.
Memorizing matters.
"Why" deserves an answer.
False praise is malpractice.
You can't teach those you don't love.
Teach them to see not what you see, but what they see.
Every discipline is a path to the deepest questions.
Poetry empowers.
Spell-check will never be good enough.

Irregular verbs are a sign of cultural vitality.
Analysis is not vivisection.
Somebody has to do the nitpicking.

What's worth waiting for

The right moment
The right word
The opportune opening
Germination
Daffodils
A child who's tying her own shoes
Opening night
Inner certainty
Clarity
Closure

Times to practice trust

When you've already told the secret
When you're already on the rappel rope

When someone else is driving
When you're feeling your way
When the end of the rope is near
When it's someone else's turn
When you have no plan
When you notice you're being guided
When you've done what you can
When you were honestly outvoted
When intuition is stronger than common sense
When the DMV licenses your daughter
When your son takes up surfing
When you've lit the candle and said the prayer